Chernobyl: The End of the Nuclear Dream

Nigel Hawkes
Geoffrey Lean
David Leigh
Robin McKie
Peter Pringle
Andrew Wilson

Illustrations by Duncan Mil

Vintage Books

A Division of Random House

New York

FIRST VINTAGE BOOKS EDITION, January 1987

Copyright © 1986 by The Observer Ltd

All rights reserved under International and Pan-American
Copyright Conventions. Published in the United States
by Random House, Inc., New York. Originally published
by Pan Books Ltd and William Heinemann Ltd, London, in 1986.

Library of Congress Cataloging in Publication Data
Chernobyl: the end of the nuclear dream.
    "Vintage specials."
    Bibliography: p.
    Includes index.
    1. Nuclear power plants—Ukraine—Chernobyl—
Accidents. I. Hawkes, Nigel.
TK1362.S65C48   1986   363.1'79   86-22462
ISBN 0-394-75107-8

            Manufactured in the United States of America
10   9   8   7   6   5   4   3   2   1

Contents

Acknowledgments

It is to an anonymous Soviet diplomat in Helsinki in the immediate aftermath of Chernobyl that we owe the observation that it was 'the worst-ever disaster in the world'. This statement, when it was publicised throughout Europe and the West, was violently disputed by the international salesmen for the nuclear industry. Six months later, it had become apparent that this assessment was perfectly correct, as far as man-made catastrophes are concerned. Information filtered out about Estonian conscripts mutinying as they were drafted to the Ukraine to work in the radioactive kitchen around the still-smouldering site of the power station. More than 135,000 Russians in the surrounding area were doused with radioactive products, it transpired, and will have to be under medical surveillance for the rest of their lives. Between 30,000 and 50,000 long-term cases of cancer are expected among them.

A study in September 1986 from the Lawrence Livermore National Laboratory in California disclosed that Chernobyl emitted as much long-term radiation into the soil, air and water of the planet as all the nuclear tests and bombs that have ever been previously exploded. The Soviet Union, after a series of laconic announcements about the disaster which only fuelled speculation, finally produced a detailed and candid assessment of the Chernobyl accident, which it delivered to the world's nuclear scientists in August 1986 at a Vienna symposium of the International Atomic Energy Authority. The findings were frightening — a series of bizarre and reckless blunders had been committed by nuclear technicians in charge of the Chernobyl plant, infected, it appeared, by the conventional wisdom of the nuclear industry, east and west, that nuclear power was 'safe'. In cash terms alone, Chernobyl is expected to have directly cost the Soviet Union more than $3 billion. The hot radioactive wreckage of the plant will have to be cooled and kept covered in concrete, literally for decades. Only a month after the accident, on 30 May, a senior Soviet official, Valentiy Falin, head of the

Novosty press agency, conceded that attitudes toward nuclear power had changed. It was clear, he said, that nuclear power was only an 'interim solution' to the energy needs of the planet. New, safer technologies would eventually have to be found. So, in those words, ended a nuclear dream — not just for the Soviet Union, but for the whole world. It was a dream that technology — and technologists — could overawe the forces of Nature herself, and provide limitless energy without paying any price.

For their assistance, some recent and much over many years, the authors would like to thank Roger Highfield of Nuclear Engineering International; James Stewart of the British Nuclear Forum; Dr Eric Voice of the Pro-Nuclear Group at Dounreay; Dr Michael Scott of Birmingham University; Dr John Dunster and Matthew Gaines of the NRPB; Prof. Edward Radford, Walter C. Patterson, the nuclear consultant; James Dalglish of the IAEA in Vienna; Peter Taylor of the Political Ecology Research Group; Colin Sweet of the Polytechnic of the South Bank, London and the senior Soviet and UN officials who paused long enough from dealing with Chernobyl to give us interviews. In the United States, thanks are due to Thomas Cochran; Stan Norris; Leonard Weiss; and William Arkin. We are grateful to James Spigelman, co-author of *The Nuclear Barons* (Michael Joseph, London, 1982) for material therein. From the London *Observer* itself, we would also like to thank many colleagues who have helped us with material and facilities, especially Simon Hoggart and Carol Keefer in Washington; Robin Lustig in Israel; and Neal Ascherson and Mark Frankland in London. Finally, we would like to thank Donald Trelford, editor of the *Observer,* for encouraging us in an arduous project.

London,
Moscow,
Washington,
October 1986

1 A small town in the Ukraine

'Thorough studies conducted in the Soviet Union have proved completely that nuclear power plants do not affect the health of the population.'

Lev Feoktistov, deputy director of the Kurchatov nuclear energy institute, 1985

Driving southwards down the M–3 road from Moscow in April 1986, a visitor from the capital would have seen the frost-burned fields of central Russia giving way at last to the green of sprouting crops.

Radishes, sorrel, spring onions and parsley would have been emerging from the country people's vegetable plots. And the decrepit single-storey rural cottages, mostly of wood and lacking all but the most primitive amenities, would have been interspersed with towns of dusty shops and pot-holed streets.

Chernobyl, in the Ukraine, is a provincial place, but not, in Russian or even in western European terms, a particularly remote one. It is about 600 km (375 miles) distant from Moscow – approximately the same distance as Turin is from Naples; New York from Cleveland, Ohio; or Hamburg from Munich. Chernobyl is also as close to its own nearest big metropolis of Kiev as say, the port of Dover is to London – no more than 150 km (80 miles).

Chernobyl was not therefore picked out from obscurity by the nuclear planners because it was far-flung. On the contrary; Chernobyl's whole attraction as a site for Soviet power station constructors was its useful proximity to big towns and big industries. They were the ones that needed electricity . . . There are 10 nuclear power plants located in the populous Ukraine, out of the 41 so far built in the Soviet Union. The biggest of all the sites is that just outside Chernobyl.

Chernobyl itself is a pretty, if dusty, town by Soviet standards, full of trees growing in the pinkish, loose soil and leafy public gardens. Here and there, a returning migrant black-and-white stork could be seen that spring, standing by its newly built nest on a rooftop, and clattering with its bill. Chernobyl has a river-port, where barges dock: here the Pripyat River is about the width of the Thames in London. Long before the nuclear power station was built, families used to go to Chernobyl for holidays and to rent rooms or cottages. There was fishing in the river and bathing in several small lakes. The power station itself was a bit of a tourist attraction, seen from across the perimeter fence – it was built on one of the prettiest spots of all, 14 km (9 miles) up the slow-running Pripyat, by what was once the little village of the same name.

The plant's own cooling-pond was more than 4 km (2½ miles) long; its banks were colonized by anglers, and the warm water – carefully monitored by Vladimir Korobeinikov, the power station's resident ecologist – supported a large fish-farm.

It was a land of lakes, sandy soil, forests and water-meadows. The nearby woods were always full of berries and wild mushrooms, which Ukrainians had gathered as usual the previous autumn, and were expected to return to gather again, as summer lengthened.

The historic town of Chernigov lay 96 km (60 miles) off to the east – a favourite for tourist bus-parties anxious to inspect its cathedral and churches. Like most Ukrainian towns and villages, it was heavily damaged during the Second World War; Hitler's armies flung themselves east-wards here in a drive to capture the strategic Soviet oilfields round Baku, only to be rolled back from a savage occupation after their defeat at Stalingrad. It was that heroic memory of the Red Army's wartime struggle which Gorbachev and other party leaders were soon to find themselves heavily invoking once again in the Ukraine.

Near the Pripyat, the soil is spongy and marshy. Stretching west and north for some 480 km (300 miles) in each direction, are the Pripet Marshes, named after the river – good duck-shooting country. They are not all swamp, however: only 16 km (10 miles) to the north, beyond the borders of the Ukraine, lay Belorussia – White Russia – whose capital is Minsk, 384 km (240 miles) to the north.

There were mixed forests and five big farms in that immediate part of the world alone, in Gomel province, around the town of Bragin. Posudovo collective farm, for example, kept 660 diary cows, and more than 1,700 animals in all. Its neighbour, the Braginsky farm, just 30 km (19 miles) out of Chernobyl, ran a large calf-rearing operation to replenish the local milk herds. The Leninsky Put farm ran 3,850 head of cattle. The nearest farm was in fact only 14 km (8 miles) away from the nuclear plant: it had more than 4,000 workers, no less than 6,500 head of cattle and another 1,500 pigs and sheep.

Altogether, there were over 100 populated farms and villages within 30 km (19 miles) of the power station, as well as the two small towns of Chernobyl and Pripyat: almost 100,000 people in total lived and worked round about. They grew flax, potatoes, maize, rapeseed, soya, and beet.

The sprawling River Dnieper ran off to the north-west, past the ancient settlement of Lyubech, feeding like the Pripyat itself into the enormous 100 km (60 miles) Kiev Reservoir, to the south, from which came the main water-supply for the city of Kiev. The sweep of the whole Dnieper basin crossed the breadbasket of the Ukraine, with its

3

steppes of oak and beech and black, fertile soil. It fed into the warm Mediterranean environs of the Black Sea.

Ukraine's capital is Kiev itself, the ancient city of two million people on a series of wooded hills on the Dnieper's right bank. Hundreds of peasants arrived there from the surrounding countryside every day to sell their produce from stalls in the famous Bessarabskiy market in Kreschatik, the Ukrainian capital's main thoroughfare – vegetables, fruit, meat and lard, milk, cottage cheese, sour cream . . . There were thousands of little street-corner stands selling ice-cream, drinking-water, fruit-juice and *pirozhki* (pancakes). The city's famous chestnut trees were just coming into blossom that April, with their candelabras of white flowers. Steamers were due to begin their regular summer excursions north up the Dnieper towards the reservoir and the Chernobyl area.

In 16 years, the power station settlement of Pripyat had become a new town in its own right, with a population of 20,000 only a few kilometres from the plant. The lorries of the construction gangs, and the heavy equipment arriving on lines of trucks at the small railway station of Yanov, were a permanent feature of the landscape – a continuous testament to the Russian search for economic growth. Some of the inhabitants had been there since the first reactor site had been cleared in 1970 with a team drafted in from the three big RBMK (Russian Graphite Moderated Channel Tube) nuclear reactors previously completed at Kursk, 350 km (200 miles) to the east. It took seven years' work to build and start up the first nuclear reactor in the Ukraine. Work promptly began on the second, then the third and the fourth on the same site. Most of the new citizens were young, with growing families: the average age at Pripyat was no more than 27. The site's official title was the 'Chernobyl atomic power station', but the workers never called it anything but 'the Pripyat station'.

Pine trees had been planted around the blocks in an attempt to soften the square monotony of Pripyat's architecture. But from the windows of their pre-fabricated apartments, the staff could rarely avoid looking out at the looming reactors and turbine halls of the power station. With its white superstructures sitting on decks of concrete, it looked rather like a ship. From its masts, grids of pylons and wires ran off south, not only towards the hungry industries of Kiev, but also towards Poland and the other Comecon states which bought Chernobyl's electricity.

Pripyat's people suffered from typical new town complaints – not enough nurseries for toddlers, no jobs for workers' wives, too many cars parked in the streets because architects had not designed garages for the subsequently affluent community. 'I'd call them teething problems,' Vladimir Voloshko, the mayor, told Soviet journalists the previous year: 'Pripyat is currently experiencing a baby boom ... We are creating new jobs for women by developing service industries.' As far as the car-parking problem was concerned, he struck an environmentalist note: 'We don't want the cars to squeeze out the people. We believe the town of Pripyat should be as safe and clean as the power plant.'

For it was an article of faith that the power plant itself was safe. Nuclear power was safe. This was a message repeated over and over again by the authorities. In 1985, the staff at the Chernobyl plant were interviewed for *Soviet Life*, an official English-language magazine for distribution in the United States to readers who were possibly sceptical after the sensational 1979 nuclear near-meltdown at the US plant at Three Mile Island. 'I wasn't afraid to take a job at a nuclear power plant,' the moustachioed 29-year-old steam turbine operator Boris Chernov assured his official interlocutors: 'There is more emotion in fear of nuclear power plants than real danger. I work in white overalls. The air is

5

clean and fresh; it's filtered most carefully.' Pyotr Bondarenko, a crew supervisor in the safety division, was even more emphatic. Working at Chernobyl, he said, was safer than driving a car:

> Robots and computers have taken over a lot of operations. None the less, the occupational safety and health agency requires that all personnel strictly abide by the rules and regulations. In order to hold a job here, you have to know industrial safety rules to perfection.

And Chernobyl's chief engineer, Nikolai Fomin, assured the world that his plant was 'completely safe' for both people and the environment. The magazine reported the reasons for his confidence:

> The huge reactor is housed in a concrete silo, and it has environmental protection systems. Even if the incredible should happen, the automatic control and safety systems would shut down the reactor in a matter of seconds. The plant has emergency core cooling systems and many other technological safety designs.

The article in *Soviet Life* kept returning to – as though preoccupied by – the question of safety. The Ukrainian power minister, Vitali Skiyerov, explained how Chernobyl was only the first instalment of nuclear power in the region. Electricity plants would soon be using their spare heat to warm the inhabitants of the Black Sea port of Odessa – 'the heat from its exhaust steam will be used in growing vegetables, fruit and mushrooms, fish and poultry farming, and irrigating fields with warm water'. He then turned to a question-and-answer session:

> QUESTION: 'Nuclear plants are being built close to big cities and resort areas. How safe are they?'

ANSWER: 'The odds of a meltdown are one in 10,000 years. The plants have safe and reliable controls that are protected from any breakdown with three safety lines. The lines operate independently without duplicating one another. New equipment with higher reliability is being developed. Pilot models are tested under conditions similar to working conditions. The environment is also securely protected. Hermetically sealed buildings, closed cycles for technological processes with radioactive agents and systems for purification and harmless waste disposal, preclude any discharge into the external environment. Nuclear plants are ecologically much cleaner than thermal plants that burn huge quantities of fossil fuel.'

Local people had not, however, abandoned their deep-seated mistrust of nuclear power stations despite these repeated official assurances of safety, and the nonchalant attitude of some of the power workers themselves. An insight into popular attitudes came in 1982, when the trade union paper *Trud* surveyed readers' letters expressing concern about the safety of nuclear power stations. The article printed a statement by a building worker at the new Smolensk plant, another RBMK design north of Chernobyl, which referred to alarmist rumours among those nearby:

It extends so far that people stop buying vegetables and fruits if they are raised in an area where a nuclear power plant is located. Could not the experts be a little more forthcoming about what goes on at these plants, so that there would be less idle conjecture?

The 'experts' were in fact by no means united. But the local people of Smolensk were not likely to have been given

7

the opportunity to read a discreet report, only found in a low-circulation philosophy journal, of what one of them had told a Soviet ecological conference two years earlier: 'Optimistic estimates of the risk fail to take into account the probability of an accident at nuclear plants, which obviously increases as the number of plants does.'

Foreign nuclear accidents – notably that at Three Mile Island – were widely covered by the Soviet media. This may have increased domestic misgivings. Certainly, some Soviet republics had resisted having nuclear power stations on their territories. It had been an unacknowledged issue in the Baltic states of Latvia and Estonia for some time, and there had been evidence in the west of disquiet about a 1,000 megawatt pressurized-water reactor (PWR) being built in the Tatar autonomous republic.

Confidence in the engineering standards at Chernobyl could scarcely have been increased by a long denunciation of the construction slippages at the site, penned in Ukrainian only three weeks earlier by a woman worker, Lyubov Kovalevska, and published in *Literaturna Ukraina*. Unrealistic building programmes were set by the authorities, she wrote. The time-scale for building a fifth reactor had been arbitrarily chopped from three years to two: 'An unrealistic programme which is not backed up by resources ... leads to disorganization of building work and often to the collapse of the plan.'

The Gorbachev regime encouraged such open criticism of subcontractors' bottlenecks and incompetence. But there was an ominous tailpiece to the litany of complaints about substandard reinforced concrete, defective fissure sealant for the nuclear waste dump, and faulty supplies of girders:

Citing these facts, I would like to draw attention to the inadmissibility of defects in the construction of nuclear power stations and power projects in general,

8

where the strength of every structure must conform to a certain standard. Every cubic metre of reinforced concrete must be a guarantee of reliability, and thus of safety.

The reference to safety was significant. For the truth was, as most of the people in the industry recognized privately, that nuclear power was potentially a very dangerous business.

On Friday 25 April, it was a spring weekend. The orchards and domestic gardens were just on the verge of bursting into masses of colour – pale green foliage, violet lilac blooms, pink cherry, white apple blossom, acacia and lilies of the valley. Many of the power station workers had taken advantage of the weather to leave town on fishing trips. Of the team of 17 responsible for repairing generating equipment at the Chernobyl No. 4 reactor, for example, no fewer than 10 were already away for the weekend. They had gone off to catch pike and listen to nightingales. One of the repair supervisors, Arkhipov, had a car and had taken it off on holiday in the depths of the Polesski region. Two others, Vladimir Lyskin and Nikolai Oleschuk, were at home in bed. So was Anatoliy Grazhdankin, the senior operator at the chemical shop. The Chernobyl plant's fire chief, 35-year-old Major Leonid Telyatnikov, was also having a day off. Not due back at the plant until the Sunday, he was at home, 6 km (4 miles) away.

It was a holiday period, in the run-up not only to the national May Day celebrations, but also to 9 May, the important public anniversary of the end of the war against Hitler. It was also the time at which No. 4 unit was being virtually shut down, for its annual fuel-change and maintenance. The night shift was, as usual, more lightly staffed than during the day. Altogether, there were probably fewer people on duty inside No. 4, than on any other evening in the life-cycle of the reactor. This may have slowed down responses to any accident: it also probably saved a lot of lives. To be at home, behind four walls, in bed in the middle of the night, was to prove, as students of civil defence in the age of nuclear war had long recognized, the least impractical way of coping with a deluge of fall-out.

There were less than 150 men in the shift that was on duty at No. 4 unit on the night of Friday, 25 April. None of them would ever forget what was to happen: and many of the men rostered for their overnight turn at the plant would never see another day of the early spring. Aleksandr Akimov was the crew supervisor, a veteran engineer. Anatoliy Kurguza was much younger: he was an operator in the vast reactor hall directly above the sealed core, who handled changes in the fuel and control rods there. Vladimir Shashionok worked on the automatic control systems. Valeriy Hodiemchuk was a basic grade operator. They were all to die quite shortly.

No. 4 unit was about 100 metres away from the adjoining No. 3 set; they shared a stubby extraction chimney, built on a monumental scale. There was another twin unit nearby, and also a vast hole in the ground. This was a building-site, running well behind schedule. It was the foundation-work for No. 5 and eventually No. 6 units, which were designed to make Chernobyl, when completed in 1988, literally the biggest power station in the world. Its planned 6,000 megawatts would be enough simultaneously to burn 6 million electric fires, or light up every house in a country the size of Britain.

Sunk into the ground behind heavy concrete containment boxes at No. 4 unit was the nuclear pile itself. It was difficult to grasp the nature of this unseen furnace merely by looking at the high, square building encasing it. Even from the instrument room of the reactor hall, towering 90 metres up, all that could be seen was a chessboard on the floor below, stretching 13 metres across, made up of hundreds of what looked like square manholes. Only the 200-tonne refuelling machine, which travelled ponderously on a crane across the hall, could ever lift those manholes under remote control and prod into the reactor's bowels, 9 metres below.

The reactor consisted of a forest of 1,600 upright metal 'pressure tubes'. Inside each of these tubes were thousands of gallons of more or less ordinary water. Its only unusual feature was that minerals and impurities were removed from the water before it was pumped into the bottom of the pipes. When the water went in, it was cold. When it came out of the top it was scaldingly hot. This simple activity was the whole purpose of nuclear power: the hot water was then converted into steam which was used to drive giant turbines, which in turn spun big electric generators.

Inside No. 4, the water was heated by clusters of uranium 'fuel rods', which ran down the middle of each pressure tube, as though they were the elements in a giant electric kettle. Each fuel rod, itself encased in metal, would have been red hot if it had been exposed to the open air. Inside it, a slow nuclear reaction was taking place. Uranium was breaking down of its own accord into other elements. Each time a change took place within an atom, a tiny amount of matter was converted, in the equations made famous by Albert Einstein, into huge bursts of pure energy. That energy was being turned into heat.

These rods, containing nearly 200 tonnes of uranium, were encased in a maze of pipework. The water could never be allowed to cease flowing through the pipes under any circumstances – it was only continuous pumping which kept the whole assembly from over-heating and turning into molten metal.

The whole piece of plumbing was in turn set in a huge

drum of graphite – a purified and precision-machined version of the blacklead in ordinary pencils – which weighed 1,700 tonnes. The drum of graphite speeded up the nuclear reaction to a useful level. It, too, would have glowed red hot if exposed to the air. Between the fuel tubes were other tubes holding 180 control rods of boron steel, which were moved up and down to slow the reaction when necessary, and keep it under control.

When the reactor was in full operation, the pressure tubes of water were not merely very hot; they were also, as their name suggests, under immense pressure – 65 times normal atmospheric pressure. The water was compressed to stop it boiling away like an ordinary kettle at 100° C. Under pressure, it could become two or three times hotter than that: welded stainless steel pipes nearly one metre across then pumped away the superheated water into large pressurized steel drums. Here it was allowed at last to vapourize into steam, which was piped into the turbine-hall, built like everything else on a gigantic scale.

The nuclear reactions inside the core did not just produce heat, of course. They also generated radioactivity. No one could venture unprotected near a reactor core once it had 'gone critical'. The graphite drum, the pressure tubes and the uranium fuel rods had all become radioactive by this time and would remain so even if the whole plant was shut down. The reactor at Chernobyl No. 4 unit accumulated about a tonne of highly radioactive 'waste' elements inside its fuel rods each year that it was in operation, some of which would remain dangerous for hundreds of years thereafter.

The inside of Chernobyl No. 4 atomic power station was thus – like every other nuclear power station in the world – a cauldron of dangerous forces. It consisted of chemicals pumped continuously under immense pressures and tremendous heat around a large mass of highly radioactive metals, in circumstances where, for human safety, it was vital that no part of the installation's contents was ever allowed to escape.

Soviet scientists and engineers – like their colleagues in the west – were confident that they had these forces imprisoned. The deputy director of the Kurchatov nuclear energy institute, Lev Feoktistov, was later asked on Soviet television what his reaction would have been had someone inquired of him on the day before Friday's events at Chernobyl, about the likelihood of a catastrophic accident at a nuclear power station. His reply was very candid: 'I would have replied that it was wholly unlikely, such an event. Wholly unlikely.'

He could scarcely have said anything else; it was Feoktistov who had co-authored the panegyric to nuclear power which had been printed the year before in the long article in *Soviet Life* about the Chernobyl plant itself. He had written:

> By the end of the next century, two-thirds of all power consumed in the world will be generated by nuclear plants . . .
>
> In the 30 years since the first Soviet nuclear power plant opened, there has not been a single instance when plant personnel or nearby residents have been seriously threatened: not a single disruption in normal operation occurred that would have resulted in the contamination of the air, water or soil.
>
> Thorough studies conducted in the Soviet Union have proved completely that nuclear power plants do not affect the health of the population.

During the night shift at Chernobyl No. 4 unit, there were what those present later described as 'muffled sounds'. There was a harsh hiss of escaping steam. At precisely 40 seconds after 1.23 a.m., a fireball appeared in the night sky over the roof of the turbine hall

The nuclear reactor at Chernobyl had just exploded.

2 Danger: radioactivity!

'The release of atom power has changed everything except our way of thinking.'

Albert Einstein

The radioactive poisons that poured from the Chernobyl plant had their origins in innocent human curiosity. By the end of the nineteenth century, physicists had begun to believe that they knew all that would ever be known about the behaviour of matter; all that remained, one of them declared, was to work out the exact values of the physical constants to four places of decimals. He could not have been more wrong. The discovery of radioactivity was to open a new and sinister chapter in man's understanding of the natural world, and just ahead lay the revolutionary discoveries by Einstein of the Special and General theories of Relativity, which were to blow the tottering structure of classical physics apart.

The trigger for the surge of new discoveries was pulled by the German physicist Roentgen, who in 1895 discovered X-rays. He realised he had hit on something extraordinary, but he did not know what it was, so he gave it the name X, the symbol usually used to denote the unknown. Asked later what he thought when he made the discovery, he replied in a phrase that would serve as the credo for many of the atomic physicists who were to follow him: 'I didn't think; I experimented.'

Inspired by Roentgen and aided by a little luck, the French physicist Henri Becquerel made an even more exciting discovery the following year. He was investigating whether materials that are naturally fluorescent could produce Roentgen's X-rays. This involved placing crystals of a salt called potassium uranyl sulphate on top of a photographic plate wrapped tightly in black paper to exclude sunlight. Becquerel then put the plates, with the crystals on top, outside on a sunny day, and found that indeed something was penetrating the black paper and darkening the plates. Next, to his frustration, came a series of cloudy days, and he left a wrapped plate, with the crystals on top, in a drawer in his laboratory. Something made him develop the plate, even though it had not been in the sun and he expected nothing. To his astonishment he found that the plate had been fogged, none the less.

What Becquerel had discovered was that his salt crystals were emitting radiation in an unending stream which did not depend on the sun, or on fluorescence. It was something like X-rays, since it could penetrate paper, but it was not quite the same. For some time, the mysterious radiation was known as Becquerel rays, until the physicist Marie Curie in 1898 came up with a name that was to stick — radioactivity. By 1901 Becquerel had determined that it was the uranium in his crystals that was the active component. A discovery had been made that was to transform physics, but more than that: it was to revolutionize the nature of warfare and become the dominant theme in the relations between the world's great powers.

Radioactivity was a wonderful toy for the scientists, who plunged into experimental programmes with feverish energy. It was not long, however, before it revealed its darker side. The first reports of injuries from X-ray work came in 1896, but it was not until 1906 that it was realized that radioactivity could also damage health. Becquerel put a vial of radium, an even more radioactive substance than uranium, in his pocket and accidentally burned his skin. Pierre Curie, interested by this phenomenon, did the same thing to himself, this time deliberately. In 1903, in a speech accepting the Nobel Prize for physics, he had warned percipiently that radioactivity 'in criminal hands' could create a burden for the human race, though he could have had no idea just how testing this burden would become.

In spite of the evidence that radioactivity was dangerous, many scientists continued to underestimate its dangers. The success of radium in treating some medical conditions – the Radium Hospital in Paris opened in 1906 – encouraged people to regard radioactivity as clean and even health-giving, able to destroy skin cancers or eliminate superfluous hair. The radioactive properties of the waters at some spas began to be advertised, and visitors were encouraged to plunge into radioactive baths, and wash down their lunches with radioactive mineral water. It is easy now to deride the early optimism and disregard for danger, though its effects still linger. The history of radiation research has been one of constantly tightening safety standards, a process which still continues today.

The first radiation workers paid a heavy price for their ignorance. Pierre Curie was knocked down and killed by a horse-drawn dray before his radium experiments had had time to do him any harm, but his wife Marie Curie eventually died from a blood cancer almost certainly initiated by her experiments. Her notebooks remain locked in a vault in Paris, too radioactive to touch. An assistant of Thomas Edison, Clarence Dally, was so seriously injured by some X-ray experiments that his hair dropped out and he developed ulcers on his head, hands and arms. They soon developed into cancers, and he died. In all, it is now estimated, some 336 of the early radiation workers died as a result of the doses they received.

What exactly was doing the damage, and what form did this damage take? To understand this it is necessary to know

An understanding of what radioactivity is followed some time after its discovery by Becquerel, and depended on a number of discoveries about the nature of the atom. Atoms are not the solid balls envisaged by nineteenth-century scientists, but are, in fact, made up of yet smaller particles, called sub-atomic particles. At the centre of the atom lies the nucleus, which is made up from two kinds of sub-atomic particles – protons, which carry a positive electrical charge, and neutrons which, as their name implies, carry no charge. Orbiting around the nucleus, rather like planets around the sun, are electrons, which carry negative electrical charges. Normally protons and electrons balance out, so that the atom as a whole is electrically neutral.

The simplest atom, hydrogen, has one proton and one electron, and no neutrons. It is the number of protons which determines what element an atom belongs to: hydrogen has one, oxygen eight, uranium 92. In addition, atoms of the same element may have differing numbers of neutrons. Having extra neutrons does not affect the chemical behaviour of an atom, but it may well affect its stability and its propensity to disintegrate and emit radiation. Different varieties of the same element are called isotopes, and are characterized by a number which represents the total number of particles (protons plus neutrons) in their nuclei. Thus uranium-235 has 92 protons and 143 neutrons, while uranium-238 has the same 92 protons, but 146 neutrons. Isotopes which are radioactive are called radio-isotopes.

more about the mysterious radiation discovered by Becquerel and the Curies. It was found to be not a single form of radiation, like X-rays, but threefold. Two forms of radiation were classified by Pierre Curie in 1900 – he called them alpha and beta rays. The same year Paul-Ulrich Villard discovered a third type, which he called gamma rays.

The three forms of radiation differed both in their nature and their properties. They were emitted when naturally unstable elements like uranium and radium decided spontaneously to change themselves into something else. In the case of alpha and beta rays, they actually represented chunks of matter which flew off during the transformation. In alpha radiation, the chunk consisted of four sub-atomic particles, two protons and two neutrons, bound together. In beta radiation, the particle was a single electron.

The third form of radiation was different, since it did not involve a particle, but was akin to a burst of pure energy, rather like X-radiation. The three types of radiation are now generally known as alpha particles, beta particles, and gamma radiation. Different transformations of radioactive elements like uranium produce different combinations of the three. For example, the commonest form of uranium, U-238, transforms itself very slowly into another element altogether, thorium-234, emitting alpha particles in the process. The thorium-234 then transforms itself, rather more briskly, into protactinium-234, emitting a beta particle. The numbers after the element's name refer to the total number of protons plus neutrons in the nucleus, or centre, of the atom.

The speed at which these transformations take place varies enormously, from fractions of a second to billions of years. If, for example, you left a piece of thorium-234 lying around, in 24 days half of it would have converted itself into protactinium-234. But, it would only take a further

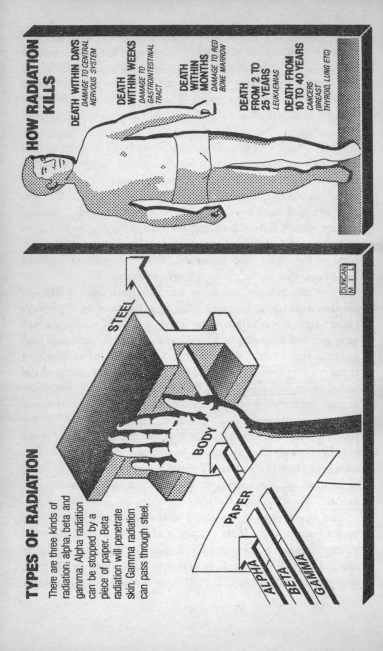

TYPES OF RADIATION

There are three kinds of radiation: alpha, beta and gamma. Alpha radiation can be stopped by a piece of paper. Beta radiation will penetrate skin. Gamma radiation can pass through steel.

ALPHA
BETA
GAMMA

PAPER

BODY

STEEL

DUNCAN MIL

HOW RADIATION KILLS

DEATH WITHIN DAYS *DAMAGE TO CENTRAL NERVOUS SYSTEM*

DEATH WITHIN WEEKS *DAMAGE TO GASTROINTESTINAL TRACT*

DEATH WITHIN MONTHS *DAMAGE TO RED BONE MARROW*

DEATH FROM 2 TO 25 YEARS *LEUKAEMIAS*

DEATH FROM 10 TO 40 YEARS *CANCERS (BREAST THYROID, LUNG ETC)*

1.17 minutes for half of that newly formed protactinium to convert itself into uranium-234. The time taken for half of any amount of a radioactive element to decay is called the half-life. If you started with 1,000 atoms of any element, after one half-life you would have only 500 left; after another half-life 250, after another 125, and so on. The rate at which this spontaneous process of radioactive decay takes place is called the activity of the element involved, and is measured in units called becquerels, abbreviated to Bq, after Henri Becquerel. One Bq represents one disintegration per second.

Radioactivity cannot be seen, smelt, or sensed by the human body, but it has profound effects. The three different kinds of radiation we have been discussing all have different energies and penetrating power, and so their effects on living things are different. Alpha particles, because they are relatively massive, are easily stopped by something as fragile as a sheet of paper, and cannot usually penetrate the dead outer layers of the skin. But if they do, through a wound or by being breathed in, they are particularly damaging. Beta particles can penetrate a centimetre or so through tissues, so can damage the skin, but not usually internal organs unless swallowed or breathed in. Gamma rays are extremely penetrating and can pass right through the body. Nothing short of a thick concrete or metal shield will stop them.

Being hit by a burst of radiation is not like walking into a wall, or being shot – there is no visible physical damage. The radiation attacks the individual cells of the body, causing the atoms that make up those cells to be altered. The change that takes place is that the atoms lose electrons and become positively charged. In this condition they are known as ions, which is why damaging forms of radiation are sometimes referred to as 'ionizing radiation', or IR. Next the ions undergo chemical changes, altering the chemistry of the cell in a way which makes it function differently, or cease to function at all. This, in turn, has biological effects on the functioning of the entire organism, which may be unnoticeable if only a few cells have been affected, or profound if many have.

It is the energy of the radiation that does the damage, and the amount of energy deposited is called the 'dose'. The amount absorbed per gram of tissue is called the 'absorbed dose' and is measured in units called rads. But this unit does not tell us how much damage is being done, because the same dose of alpha particles is more damaging than beta particles. To take account of this the dose must be weighted to make allowance for its damage potential; it is then known as the 'dose equivalent' and is measured in rems. Even this is not quite enough, because it fails to take account of the fact that some organs of the body are more susceptible than others. To allow for this, further weighting factors must be introduced, to produce an 'effective dose equivalent' also measured in rems. (To make an already complex situation yet more difficult, radiobiologists have recently devised themselves new units, the gray (Gy) and the sievert (Sv). One gray is equal to 100 rads, and one sievert equal to 100 rems.)

Mankind is exposed to many sources of radiation, some natural and some man-made. In normal life, by far the most significant is the natural background radiation, from the sun and from terrestrial sources – rocks, soils and the radioactive gas radon which is found in the air. Such doses vary from place to place, but as a generalization it is fair to say that 80 per cent of the radiation received by individuals comes from these natural sources.

Among the man-made sources, by far the most significant is the medical use of X-rays. Second, but very much smaller, is the fall-out of radioactive particles produced by nuclear weapon testing in the atmosphere – now banned by international treaty, but still leaving a lingering burden of long half-life radioactive materials in the environment. The amount of radioactivity in the environment from the normal operation of nuclear power stations is smaller still, with further contributions from miscellaneous sources such as luminous watches, TV sets, and air travel – getting above some of the protective layer of the atmosphere increases the dose of cosmic radiation.

This picture of the radiation burden is a relatively reassuring one, often used by nuclear power proponents to demonstrate how safe nuclear plants are. If X-rays, which everybody recognizes as a beneficial use of radiation so long as it is subject to proper controls, contribute overwhelmingly more than nuclear power, then is it reasonable to express anxieties about the operation of power plants? In a perfect world, it is an argument that might carry conviction. But as the Chernobyl disaster was to demonstrate, this is far from a perfect world. Rather it is one in which human fallibility and the propensity of machines to go wrong must be taken into account.

The inside of a nuclear reactor contains large amounts of many dangerous radioactive elements. How much depends on how long the reactor has been working, for it is the products of the process of nuclear fission, not the initial charge of uranium fuel, which present the greatest hazards. As the uranium fuel fissions, it produces a complex mixture of the radioactive forms of many elements – known as radio-isotopes – inside the fuel elements.

The effect of any one of these isotopes, if it were to be released, depends on a number of variables – its activity, its half-life, what happens to it when taken up by the body, and how quickly it is excreted, and so on. One critical radio-isotope, for example, is iodine-131, both because it is relatively volatile and therefore likely to escape in an accident, and also because it is quickly taken up by the thyroid gland.

Fortunately it has a relatively short half-life of only eight days. At the other extreme is plutonium-239, a highly toxic radio-isotope with a half-life of 24,400 years. Although much less volatile than iodine-131, and hence less likely to escape, plutonium-239 is dangerous because once it is taken up by the body it is excreted very slowly and can be assumed to remain in the body for the rest of the life-span, continuing to irradiate the tissues with alpha particles. Other radio-isotopes of particular concern include strontium-90 and caesium-137, both beta emitters.

In 1945, when nuclear fission had just demonstrated its awesome power over Hiroshima and Nagasaki, and the first nuclear reactors for plutonium production were being built in Britain, biologists were faced with the question of setting safety standards. The dangers of radiation were known, though they had hitherto been a problem for a small community of specialists who had first met in 1921 to fix what they called 'tolerance doses' – those levels of radio-activity which could be tolerated without harm. When war broke out in 1939, the total world stock of radium, then the only widely used radioactive isotope, amounted to a mere three kilograms. By 1945, with the success of the Manhattan Project to build the atomic bombs, a totally new world had been created. An unprecedented increase in the amounts of radioactivity produced by man was about to take place and new standards were needed – though, at that time, as the official historian of the British nuclear programmes, Margaret Gowing, drily remarks, 'It does not appear that anyone seriously envisaged the problem implied by an indefinite expansion of nuclear programmes of all kinds.'

The raw material from which a much greater understanding of radiation biology could be gleaned was already at hand – the case histories of the hapless victims of the bombing of Hiroshima and Nagasaki. Within the first three seconds after the two bombs exploded, hundreds of thousands died as a result of blast and heat. Those who survived the first moments became the guinea pigs for establishing radiation standards which still for the most part apply today.

Those who studied the pattern of death among the survivors of the initial explosion established that there are five successive 'waves' of death, each affecting a larger population than the one before. The successive waves may overlap with one another to some extent.

The first deaths occur almost immediately among people exposed to very high levels of radiation. The radiation overwhelms their central nervous systems, leading to death within hours, or even minutes. Those exposed to rather lower levels of radiation escape this fate, only to die from gastro-intestinal damage in the week or two following the exposure. The symptoms include anorexia, nausea, vomiting, diarrhoea, intestinal cramps, salivation, dehydration and loss of weight. When combined with symptoms such as fatigue, apathy, sweating, fever, headache and hypotension, these have sometimes been given the title 'radiation sickness'.

The third wave of death consists of those who avoid gastro-intestinal injury, or even recover from it, only to perish a month or two after exposure from damage to the bone marrow, the tissue responsible for forming blood. If too many bone marrow cells have been destroyed, the symptoms include bleeding under the skin, in the mouth, and in the internal organs. The loss of white blood cells makes the body particularly susceptible to infections.

At the time of Hiroshima, little could be done for patients in this category. But since the advent of bone marrow transplant operations, it may be possible to save many lives by replacing the destroyed bone marrow. The Chernobyl disaster has provided the first opportunity to test whether this will succeed, but it is too early yet to know.

These three waves of so-called 'early' deaths are followed by two more, of fatal cancers, which will claim the lives of many more. It is this category which provides by far the largest number of deaths, but they are much less easy to attribute unequivocally to the radiation exposure. This is because many people die of cancer anyway, and the types of cancer caused by radiation are indistinguishable from those occurring naturally.

First will come the leukaemias, particularly in children. The first of these that are due to the Chernobyl disaster will be detected in a couple of years' time, and the deaths will reach a peak in a decade or so, before slowly declining and finally tailing off about 25 years from now. Just as the leukaemias pass their peak, the final wave will be beginning to rise − cancers of the breast and thyroid, of the lung, stomach, liver, large intestine, bone, oesophagus, small intestine, urinary bladder, pancreas, rectum and lymphatic tissues, in roughly that order of frequency. Nobody knows when that wave will pass, but the numbers are likely to go on rising until at least the year 2025.

The experience from Hiroshima is not a particularly encouraging one. Today, more than 40 years after the bomb exploded, people exposed to it are still developing cancers and indeed the excess risk of cancer among survivors is still increasing. So on the basis of that experience Chernobyl will still be killing people 40 years from now, in the year 2026.

How many people, and which people, are questions that cannot be answered exactly, because of two sources of uncertainty. The first is the fact that people differ quite strikingly in their response to irradiation, some showing a sensitivity two to three times greater than others. The second is that the evidence carefully accumulated from Hiroshima, and used to set the radiation limits for exposure of workers and of the population in general, may be misleading. There is a growing certainty among radiobiologists that the levels are too high by a factor of at least two.

Hiroshima was not a controlled experiment, but an act of war. Using its death statistics to calculate how dangerous radioactivity is involves making assumptions about the amount of radioactivity survivors were exposed to. The bomb that destroyed Hiroshima in 1945 ('Little Boy' it was called by the scientists, in an apparent reference to Franklin D. Roosevelt) was a uranium bomb encased in a steel tube three metres long and less than a metre in diameter, weighing four tonnes. It was the only bomb of its type that has ever been exploded. (The Nagasaki bomb – or 'Fat Man', a reference to Winston Churchill – was a plutonium bomb.)

Nobody knew then, or has been able to discover since, exactly what pattern and intensity of radiation Little Boy produced. After the war no identical bombs were built and tested to provide the data needed to make sense of the Hiroshima casualty figures. What was done was to make estimates of the likely radiation intensities at different distances from ground zero. It is these estimates – really little better than informed guesses – which have hitherto formed the basis for radiation standards.

More recently the Americans have built a replica of Little Boy – not to explode it, but to run it in a controlled way rather like a nuclear reactor, and to measure the radiation that emerged from the bomb's casing in the split second before it exploded. What they found was the steel casing of the bomb soaked up much of the radiation, and that less radiation came out of the end of the bomb than out of the sides. At the moment of detonation, the bomb was tilted at an angle of fifteen degrees, so that its radiation was unevenly spread. They also realized that the weather was humid, and therefore soaked up more of the radiation than previously allowed for.

Finally, they had another look at the protection given to bomb survivors who were indoors at the time of the explosion. Old Hiroshima was lightly built, its houses consisting of wood and paper, and they gave little protection from the radiation. But, when the studies were looked at again, scientists realized they had underestimated the amount of protection given by the fact that the houses huddle together. Computer simulations show that the radiation weakens as it passes successively through several flimsy houses.

The results of these experiments are not yet complete, but it is clear that they will revise our view quite dramatically about the amount of radiation reaching the victims. It seems likely, the Chairman of the study indicated in an interview with BBC Television shown on *Panorama* on 12 May 1986, to influence radiation standards 'in a rather severe way'. The conclusion will be that the people now dying of cancer in Japan received only half as much radiation as has hitherto been believed. And that means that radiation must be twice as dangerous as present-day standards suggest.

Some radiobiologists would go further in tightening standards, so as to take account of those who are particularly sensitive to radiation. Dr Edward Radford, a former Chairman of the US Committee on Radiation Effects and for many years a campaigner for tighter standards, believes that a further factor of three should be built in to take account of these people, who may amount to as much as 10 per cent of the population. He would add a further factor of two to allow for the fact that many cancers are induced which do not kill; at the moment, only deaths from cancer are considered. If Radford is right, that would imply a tightening of radiation standards by a factor of at least ten – but not all radiobiologists accept his analysis.

The new evidence about Hiroshima may help explain one of the mysteries about cancer incidence among those working with uranium in mines in Canada, Czechoslovakia and the United States. Uranium miners are exposed to radiation every day, and provide a population whose health can be followed closely. The studies have shown that even allowing for the different type of radiation involved, the miners are between four and seven times more likely to get cancer than the bomb survivors, when they are exposed to the same dose. At least part of this discrepancy could be accounted for by the fact that the bomb survivors' dose has been consistently overestimated. In reality, the uranium miners have received a greater dose than the matching bomb survivors, and it is no wonder that they have developed more cancers.

Establishing safe standards has been a preoccupation among radiobiologists for more than 50 years. The trend has been towards tighter and tighter standards. As Professor Karl Morgan, for many years a member of the International Commission on Radiological Protection, points out, 'When I began this work 50 years ago, we were not concerned much about the effects of radiation on man and many of the people felt that a little radiation was probably good for you.' Margaret Gowing records how British standards for external radiation were reduced progressively from 1.5 roentgens a week in 1924 (1 roentgen is equal to 0.9 rems) to 1.0 in 1934, 0.5 in 1936, 0.3 in 1950 and 0.1 in 1956. The standards in the early years were almost certainly dangerously high, but the number of radiation workers was small and the general public faced no risk at all.

What changed the attitude was both a growing understanding of the dangers, and the vast growth in the development of nuclear energy and the use of radioactive materials. For the first time the radiobiologists had to grapple with the problems posed by the potential release of the massive quantities of radioactive material in the core of a nuclear reactor – which until the Chernobyl disaster was to remain only a theoretical possibility – and with the more routine question of setting standards for routine releases during reactor operations and fuel reprocessing.

Analysis of the problem showed that of the many potential dangers from radioactive releases, there was usually one particular isotope that presented the greatest danger. Among possible gaseous releases, for example, iodine-131 is dangerous because it might be deposited on grass, eaten by cows, appear in their milk, and then be dangerous to children because they drink a lot of milk and their thyroid glands, where iodine is concentrated, are still growing and are thus likely to take up more of the iodine-131 from the milk. Thus in the immediate aftermath of an accident in which iodine-131 has been released, as at Windscale in 1957 and at Chernobyl in 1986, efforts must be made to break this 'critical pathway' either by destroying milk, or by providing iodine as a prophylactic to groups at risk to saturate their thyroids with normal iodine and prevent them taking up the dangerous radioactive form. Since iodine-131 has only a short half-life, the danger it presents, though acute, does not persist for long.

The other radio-isotopes that present a significant hazard include krypton, xenon, strontium, caesium and plutonium. The krypton isotopes are mostly short-lived, but because krypton is a gas, they present hazards immediately after release; within a day they have become relatively insignificant. Strontium-89 and -90, with half-lives of 52.7 days and 27.7 years respectively, are a hazard because they are concentrated naturally in the bone, in place of the calcium normally present. Xenon is a gas, so is likely to escape, and at least six of the eight xenon isotopes present represent an immediate hazard. Within 24 hours, however, only xenon-133 whose half-life is 5.27 days continues to be a serious danger. Two caesium isotopes, caesium-134 and -137, with half-lives of just over two years, and 30 years respectively, are a hazard because they tend to concentrate in muscle tissue.

Typically, a 1,000-megawatt reactor which has been operating for several years and has thus reached a stable plateau will contain something of the order of 10,000 million curies of radioactivity. (A megawatt of electricity is sufficient to run a thousand single-bar, one-kilowatt electric fires.) Converting this into becquerels, the units used in this book, involves multiplying by 3.7×10^{10}, so that the total inventory is equal to 3.7×10^{20} – or, to spell it out in full, 370,000,000,000,000,000,000 Bq. This is obviously a very large quantity of radioactivity indeed, and it is worthwhile to compare it with the fission product yield of a small atomic bomb.

The comparison is not altogether straightforward, because one of the major sources of radiation produced by a bomb are the neutrons also generated by the fission process. But, after the first minute, essentially all the remaining material from the explosion has risen so high into the atmosphere that neutrons no longer reach the ground, and what is left are fission products that gradually fall to earth as 'fall-out'. Taking a 1 kiloton fission bomb (a very small bomb, only a twelfth of the yield of the weapon which destroyed Hiroshima), the total radioactivity of the 300 or so isotopes of 36 different elements produced in the explosion one minute after ignition would be about 30,000 million curies, or three times the total inventory of the 1,000-megawatt reactor.

Within a day, the comparison looks slightly different. Radiation from the bomb will have fallen off very rapidly, to about one two-thousandth of its one-minute value, while the radioactivity from the nuclear reactor will have declined by only a factor of about five.

Such comparisons are interesting, though not very meaningful in real terms, because nobody supposes that even the most appalling accident to a nuclear plant could release the entire inventory, while a bomb is obviously a highly efficient way of dispersing all its fission products into the atmosphere.

None the less, even a partial release of the gaseous and volatile parts of the inventory amounts to a very large quantity of radioactivity. One of the earliest attempts to assess the consequences was carried out in 1956 for the US Atomic Energy Commission (AEC) by Brookhaven National Laboratory. It was called *Theoretical Possibilities and Consequences of Major Accidents in Large Nuclear Power Plants*, but is normally referred to as the *Brookhaven Report*, or more familiarly by its AEC code, *WASH-740*. It dealt with the possibility of an accident to a 200-megawatt nuclear reactor – about one-fifth the size of the Chernobyl reactor – and adopted as the basis for its worst-case analysis the AEC's 'maximum credible accident' – the release of 50 per cent of the inventory of radioactive isotopes. It assumed that the plant was built 30 miles from a city.

The results of *WASH-740* showed that the worst possible accident, in the least favourable weather conditions, would produce 3,400 deaths and 43,000 injuries, property damage of $7,000 million (at 1956 prices, remember) and contamination of a land area the size of Maryland. People would die at distances up to 15 miles away from the plant, and be injured up to 45 miles away.

This report was unpalatable to the AEC, which at the time was trumpeting the virtues of nuclear electricity. It suggested very clearly that the potential costs of a catastrophic accident would be far more than any electrical utility, or any insurance company, would be able to bear.

One consequence was the passage in 1957 by Congress of the Price-Anderson Act, designed to protect the nuclear industry from liability in the event of such an accident. The act set a limit of $560 million in payments for a nuclear accident, $500 million provided by Federal funds and another $60 million through insurance policies funded by the industry. Clearly, if *WASH-740* was anything like right, and the unthinkable did happen, these funds would be nothing like sufficient to meet legitimate claims. But the industry was not deterred.

In 1964, perhaps hoping for a more palatable result, the AEC commissioned an update to *WASH-740*. But the results were even more alarming. The results finally came to light in 1973, when a Chicago lawyer threatened to sue the AEC unless it published the suppressed report; it emerged that the update of *WASH-740* had calculated that the worst imaginable accident would kill 45,000 people, injure 100,000, contaminate an area the size of Pennsylvania and do $17,000 million worth of damage to property (at 1965 prices).

By the time this very pessimistic report had finally seen the light of day, a number of other studies had been published. One of the best known was carried out by Professor Norman Rasmussen of Massachusetts Institute of Technology, who was charged with looking into the whole subject of nuclear reactor safety. His conclusions on the likely consequences of the worst possible accident were very much more reassuring than *WASH-740* or its update. The worst possible conclusions, he said, were 3,300 deaths, 45,000 illnesses, and 1,500 fatal cancers which would appear decades later. The area of radiation effects would be 290 square miles, and the cost $14,000 million.

At about the same time, a British expert, F. R. Farmer of the Safety and Reliability Directorate of the United Kingdom Atomic Energy Authority, published his own estimates of the likely results of a severe accident at a hypothetical 480-megawatt plant situated in a rural area but with a town of a few thousand people a few miles away, and a million people living within 20–30 miles – circumstances fairly typical of reactor-siting policy in Britain. Farmer assumed that the reactor inventory was 4,000 million curies of volatile and gaseous fission products, and that a tenth of the iodine (5 million curies) and of the caesium (500,000 curies) escaped.

In addition to prompt deaths in the immediate vicinity of the plant – a relatively small proportion of the total – Farmer estimated that the chances were that such an accident would cause 1,000 cases of thyroid cancer within a 60-mile radius within 20 years. In addition, inhalation of caesium-137 would produce about 50 leukaemias or other cancers, and a similar number of lung cancers might be caused by the inhalation of ruthenium. Casualties could be higher, Farmer admitted, depending on the wind direction, and he quoted a 20 per cent chance that the number would lie between 1,000 and 10,000, from cancers of the thyroid. Equally he pointed out that if the reactor were on a coastal site (as many of Britain's reactors are) and there was a 50 per cent chance of the wind blowing out to sea, then casualties might be very much lower.

In 1979 the British Nuclear Installations Inspectorate (NII) produced rather different estimates in the course of preparing a report on the safety of pressurized water reactors (PWR), then (as now) proposed for introduction into Britain. Its worst-case analysis suggested that more than 30,000 people would die in a PWR accident in Britain, most of the casualties being cancer deaths occurring many years later. The figure was not published in the official version of the report: like the AEC 15 years earlier, the NII flinched at the prospects of headlines saying '30,000 will die in worst nuclear disaster'.

The NII study concluded that less serious accidents in PWRs would cause about ten times as many deaths in more densely populated Britain than they would in the United States. In the worst possible accident considered, in which all the volatile material in the reactor escaped, in the most densely populated PWR site, and where the weather conditions were the most unfavourable, 1,500 people would be killed soon after the accident, and another 30,000 would develop cancer later in life. If the same accident were to happen at the least populated site there would be 200 early deaths and 10,000 cancer deaths. More favourable weather conditions would reduce casualties greatly, with cancer deaths falling to between 1,000 and 8,000, depending on the site of the reactor.

But Mr John Dunster, Director of Nuclear Safety at the Health and Safety Executive at the time, who was responsible for the study, said that the worst accident that should be considered for planning purposes would be the release of one per cent of the volatile material in the core – which would kill between 30 and 3,000 people in Britain, depending on the detailed circumstances.

These wide discrepancies make it clear that it is the underlying assumptions about the proportion of inventory released, the wind direction and speed, and the proximity of large centres of population which determine the final figures. The impact of the figures depends on whether the studies choose to quote worst-case scenarios, which may be quite improbable, or like Farmer to offer a number of conclusions based on different assumptions. Of course, whichever the author of the report chooses to do, it is the worst-case analysis which tends to figure in the newspaper headlines.

In 1980, after the Three Mile Island accident in which only one ten-thousandth of the radioactive iodine in the reactor escaped into the environment, the US Nuclear Regulatory Commission (NRC) (the successor to the AEC as licensor of nuclear plants) commissioned a follow-up to the Rasmussen study. This was carried out by Sandia National Laboratories in New Mexico, and used a computer model to calculate a wide variety of possible accident consequences. Demographic, meteorological and economic data were compiled for each of the 80 sites in the United States where nuclear plants were operating or under construction.

The study, begun in the immediate wake of the accident, took two years. It emphasized how greatly the consequences of an accident can vary, depending on wind, rain, the speed of the response to the emergency and the population distribution around the plant. The worst-case scenario postulated core damage in the reactor, melting of the fuel, failure of all safety systems and a major breach in the reactor containment allowing a large release of radioactivity into the atmosphere. The probability of such an accident was put at one per 100,000 reactor years.

The consequences of such an accident were then calculated for all 80 sites, with different assumptions made for weather and evacuation of people from the area. In the very worst case, which assumed a rainfall carrying the radioactive plume straight down on to a population centre, total casualties could exceed 100,000 and damage could exceed $300,000 million. The final version of the report published by the NRC did not contain these figures, but quoted average figures which were very much lower. But the worst-case figures were made public by Democratic Congressman Edward J. Markey, who gave them to the *Washington Post*.

The figures were embarrassing to the NRC because unlike earlier studies they dealt with real reactors on real sites. The computer predicted that the highest death toll would occur if the worst-case accident happened at the Salem nuclear plant on the Delaware River. Wilmington, Delaware, 20 miles north of the plant, would suffer most of the casualties. The greatest property damage would occur if the accident took place at Indian Point 3 reactor, 25 miles north of New York City on the Hudson River. A total of $314,000 million in damages could result from such an accident.

The NRC responded to Markey by pointing out that the worst-case scenario implied two unlikely events – a reactor accident with a probability of one in 100,000, and weather conditions with a probability of one in 10,000. Combining the two probabilities meant that the chances of such an accident happening were in fact one in a thousand million.

In general terms the most important factor identified by the study in determining the toll from a nuclear accident is whether people who live near it are clustered in towns, and whether the plant is within 25 miles of a big city. 'Irrespective of size, population centres beyond 25 miles do not contribute to early fatalities' the report said. In some cases, the maximum distance from the plant at which there would be early fatalities would be 13 miles. But if there were towns or cities 10 to 20 miles from nuclear plants, the number of early fatalities in a really bad accident might increase and even under favourable conditions could be twice as high as it would be when the population was more spread out.

The report also concluded that prompt evacuation of people living within a 10-mile radius of nuclear plants could reduce significantly the number dying. It doubted, however, if the evacuation plans prepared for emergencies in the United States were capable of achieving very much.

All these figures refer to early deaths, those occurring within a few weeks or months of the accident. To them must be added those caused by cancers, which also vary widely according to geography and weather. In the case of the Salem plant, for example, an additional 40,000 cancer deaths were predicted. For most of the reactor sites studied, cancer deaths exceed early deaths, sometimes by a wide margin. In the case of the plant at Ginna, Ontario, for example, 2,000 early deaths are predicted, but 14,000 cancer deaths.

Studies of possible disasters invariably deal with the danger of cancer in terms of probabilities – something of a puzzle to the public, to whom cancer is a disease you either have or haven't got. The disaster at Chernobyl, if it is properly monitored and if sufficient detailed information is released by the Soviet authorities, will provide data to put those probabilities on a much firmer foundation. No previous accident has produced such an unambiguous and massive release, though there is a growing suspicion that much smaller releases from power stations and from the Windscale reprocessing plant in the UK, have been the cause of some cancer deaths. These are the mysterious 'clusters' of leukaemia deaths among children living close to the plants. The figures show, for example, that children under the age of 10 living in Seascale, a village just over a mile from Windscale, have ten times as great a chance of suffering from leukaemia as do children of a similar age in the population as a whole. The total number of leukaemias involved is small (less than ten) but the statistics are striking, and since the Windscale cluster came to light other areas in Britain have been found with similarly elevated levels. Some are near nuclear plants (at Berkeley in Gloucestershire, Leiston near Sizewell in Suffolk and at Dounreay in the north of Scotland), but others seem to have no connection with radioactivity. There is one in Slough, Berkshire, for example, and another in the village of Dane End, Essex, neither of which is close to a nuclear plant.

A recent investigation was carried out into the Windscale cluster by Sir Douglas Black, who headed a committee of experts appointed by the Ministry of Health. It concluded that the cluster was real, that it was 'unusual but not unique' and that the suggestion that it was linked with an increased level of radioactivity 'is by no means proven'. But the argument used was a curious one, to say the least. Using existing estimates about the dangers of radioactivity, it calculated that excess radiation from Windscale (estimated as 13 per cent above background) would have given rise to only 0.091 leukaemia deaths. In fact there were 3.5 'excess' deaths to explain. Sir Douglas concluded simply that the doses received were insufficient to account for the deaths, and therefore did not support the view that radioactivity was responsible.

It now seems likely since the 1950s the children were exposed to much higher levels. British Nuclear Fuels, who run the Windscale plant, have admitted that Sir Douglas and his committee were by mistake given the wrong figures for uranium released from the plant in the 1950s. Instead of the half kilogram he assumed, it seems likely that at least 20 kilograms were released. This could explain the discrepancy – or, alternatively, it may be that the children who suffered were much more radiation-sensitive than average. In any event, it remains a question that needs an answer, as Sir Douglas himself conceded in his report, which recommended further studies.

The deaths investigated by Sir Douglas had all taken place close to the Windscale plant. But in the scenarios of nuclear catastrophe which came true at Chernobyl, most of the delayed deaths may well occur a long way from the plant. In the close confines of Europe where national boundaries are never far away, it is likely that any large accident will send its plume of radioactivity over neighbouring countries, where it will claim victims many years later. Nuclear power has meant that nations cannot even keep their disasters to themselves – as Chernobyl was to prove to a bewildered and unprepared Politburo in Moscow.

But the pressure to build a nuclear world was one that the institutions of the planet had no way of resisting when – 30 years ago – engineers and soldiers started to pursue their own dreams.

3 Building a nuclear world

'Nuclear power is the safest form of energy yet known to man.'

> UK energy minister Peter Walker, the month before
> Chernobyl, 16 March 1986

'Man has not grown up enough to be trusted with nuclear reactors.'

> New Zealand Nobel prizewinner, Sir George Porter

On 2 December 1942, a group of scientists completed construction of a strange edifice inside an old squash court at Chicago University. Their handiwork consisted of 6 tonnes of uranium, 50 tonnes of uranium oxide, and 400 tonnes of graphite. It was an odd-looking complex – with a very unusual purpose. The team had, in fact, built the world's first nuclear reactor.

At 2.20 p.m. the researchers' leader Enrico Fermi, carefully removed the reactor's control rods – and so initiated the world's first self-sustaining nuclear fission reaction. The atomic age had begun.

It was an historic moment, for it showed that humans could tap and control the vast energies which scientists had just discovered within the atom. Many senior researchers had argued that this would prove to be impossible. Even Nobel prizewinner Lord Rutherford, one of the pioneers of nuclear research, once dismissed the prospect of harnessed nuclear energy as 'moonshine'.

More importantly, the reactor's construction tied the nuclear industry, from its birth, to the military. The Chicago plant was constructed in complete secrecy and was later used as the prototype of the Hanford reactors which produced plutonium for the atomic bomb that later destroyed Nagasaki on 9 August 1945. Since then, the nuclear industry's military link has hung like a millstone round its neck. It has imbued its controllers with a paranoid sense of secrecy and, in turn, this has intensified the fears of many people who now consider reactors to be little more than atomic bombs encased in concrete.

The Chernobyl disaster was only to increase those fears. Nevertheless, the nuclear industry has not always been so reviled. When the Allied forces dropped the Hiroshima and Nagasaki atom bombs, a stunned world was suddenly made aware of a force with seemingly unlimited potential. Very quickly politicians and scientists were dreaming that it could be used to solve the world's energy problems.

'This new force offers enormous possibilities for improving public welfare, for revamping our industrial methods, and for increasing the standard of living,' said American lawyer, James Newman who helped draft the United States Atomic Energy Act in 1946. Some enthusiasts even claimed that nuclear power would become 'too cheap to meter'.

Such optimism was understandable. The energy contained in a one kilogram (2.2 lb) lump of uranium, when used in a nuclear reactor, releases energy equivalent to that provided by the burning of 3,000 tonnes of coal in a conventional power plant. The necessary technology is based on those crucial discoveries which began in the late nineteenth century and which increased in pace during the heady days of the late 1930s when the final crucial breakthroughs were made. The most important of these was the realization that certain very unstable atoms could be made to disintegrate in a runaway fashion. This process is called fission.

In nuclear fission, an atom – such as a uranium atom – is struck by a neutron which splits it apart. From the debris smaller atoms are formed, energy is released, and – crucially – so are other spare neutrons. These neutrons strike other atoms, causing them to split apart and release even more energy. In this way vast amounts of energy can be released. The first atomic bombs had the explosive force of 20,000 tonnes of TNT. Later bombs have been made with the explosive forces of several million tonnes – each enough to lay waste to one of the world's largest cities.

But these titanic releases of energy can also be harnessed in a manageable form. Inside nuclear reactors, fission is controlled and energy is released slowly. The underlying process is simple. Uranium is first placed inside long metal canisters, and these are then slotted into a reactor's core which, at Chernobyl, was made of graphite. This graphite acts as a 'moderator'. It slows down the neutrons that are emitted by the disintegrating uranium atoms. These neutrons normally fly out at speeds too fast for interaction with other uranium atoms and must be slowed down if nuclear fission is to take place.

Control rods, usually made of boron steel (which absorbs neutrons) are also slotted into the core. Nuclear fission cannot take place while these rods are inside the core. However, as they are slowly removed, fission can begin and heat is produced. By moving the rods in and out of a reactor, operators can carefully control neutron flow and heat production. To take away the heat, a gas or a liquid – known as a coolant – is pumped through the core. The coolant gets heated – depending on the type of reactor – to between 250 and 600 °C and is then used to turn water into very hot steam. The steam drives a turbine which produces electricity.

All reactors have this basic design, though there are many variants on it. French, American and Russian reactors use water as coolant, British reactors use gas. Some use uranium for fuel, others a mixture of uranium and plutonium. Today

Reactors operational, under construction and planned, as of the end of 1985

Country	Operational Units	Under construction Units	Planned Units	Nuclear generated electricity in 1985 % of total
Argentina	2	1	3	10.1
Austria	1	—	—	—
Belgium	8	—	—	59.8
Brazil	1	1	7	1.7
Bulgaria	4	2	2	31.6
Canada	16	6	1	12.7
China	—	1	2	—
Cuba	—	2	—	—
Czechoslovakia	5	11	—	14.6
Egypt	—	—	2	—
Finland	4	—	—	38.2
France	43	19	4	64.8
FR Germany	19	6	10	31.2
German DR	5	6	—	12.0
Hungary	2	2	2	23.6
India	6	4	4	2.4
Iran	—	2	—	—
Iraq	—	—	1	—
Israel	—	—	1	—
Italy	3	3	6	3.8
Japan	33	11	4	22.4
Korea, Republic of	4	5	4	25.9
Libya	—	—	2	—
Mexico	—	2	—	—
Netherlands	2	—	2	6.1
Pakistan	1	—	1	0.9
Philippines	—	1	—	—
Poland	—	2	4	—
Romania	—	3	2	—
South Africa	2	—	—	4.1
Spain	8	2	5	24.0
Sweden	12	—	—	42.3
Switzerland	5	—	—	39.8
Taiwan	6	—	4	53.1
Thailand	—	—	1	—
Turkey	—	—	1	—
UK	38	4	1	19.8
USA	93	26	2	15.5
USSR	51	34	39	10.3
Yugoslavia	1	—	1	5.4
Total	375	156	116	18.3

Source: *Nuclear Engineering International, 1986.*

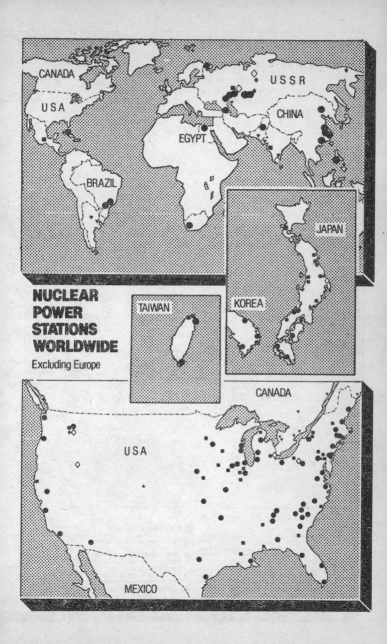

NUCLEAR
POWER
STATIONS
WORLDWIDE

Excluding Europe

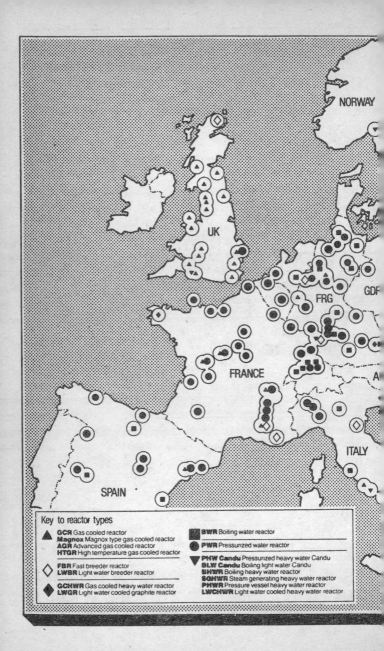

Key to reactor types

GCR Gas cooled reactor
Magnox Magnox type gas cooled reactor
AGR Advanced gas cooled reactor
HTGR High temperature gas cooled reactor

FBR Fast breeder reactor
LWBR Light water breeder reactor

GCHWR Gas cooled heavy water reactor
LWGR Light water cooled graphite reactor

BWR Boiling water reactor

PWR Pressurized water reactor

PHW Candu Pressurized heavy water Candu
BLW Candu Boiling light water Candu
BHWR Boiling heavy water reactor
SGHWR Steam generating heavy water reactor
PHWR Pressure vessel heavy water reactor
LWCHWR Light water cooled heavy water reactor

NUCLEAR POWER STATIONS IN EUROPE

Sites showing 50 mile radius risk areas

FINLAND

EDEN

USSR

POLAND

CHERNOBYL

HUNGARY

RUMANIA

YUGOSLAVIA

BULGARIA

TURKEY

DUNCAN
MIL

there are 375 nuclear reactors operating in 26 countries round the world. They produce about 18 per cent of the planet's electricity. For an energy source that is only 44 years old that represents an astonishing growth.

However, most post-war nuclear enthusiasm concentrated mainly on the use of reactors for atomic weapons construction. The first reactors, built in France, the United States, the Soviet Union and Britain, were for military purposes only. These nuclear installations were built to take advantage of the remarkable changes that occur when uranium is placed inside a reactor's core. Uranium, which has usually first undergone a difficult enrichment process, breaks down under a constant neutron bombardment. The first crucial product is heat. But there are other effects. The most important of these – at least to bomb makers – is the production of plutonium.

Plutonium does not exist in nature and can only be made artificially. However, it is particularly useful for making nuclear bombs. As a result, the first reactors were designed and built only to turn uranium into plutonium. The massive amounts of heat they produced were viewed by the military designers as an inconvenience. Other by-products are also produced and are decidedly less welcome. Inside a reactor, uranium breaks down into many different, lighter elements, such as strontium, caesium, and krypton. Often these products are in a highly radioactive state and emit streams of dangerous particles, including alpha, beta, gamma and neutron radiation.

The metal fuel cladding that surrounds uranium fuel pins is sufficient to contain the alpha and beta radiation, but thick concrete shielding is necessary to block the gamma rays and neutrons. Without this protection, plant operators would quickly sicken and die of radiation poisoning. Such measures highlight the disadvantage of nuclear energy. It produces deadly, invisible radiation that must be tightly

One of the most important processes in the nuclear fuel cycle is uranium enrichment.

Uranium occurs naturally in the mineral pitchblende, a black, crumbly mineral, mined mainly in the United States, Canada, Australia, and South Africa. This natural uranium exists in two different forms. These two forms – or isotopes as they are properly known – are chemically identical, although only one, which is called uranium-235, supports fission. However, only about 0.7 per cent of uranium is made up of uranium-235, so its levels in nuclear fuel usually have to be artificially increased, or 'enriched'.

Enrichment is an immensely complex and very expensive procedure because the two isotopes are chemically identical. It is carried out in special separation plants, usually by forcing uranium atoms through very thin, porous membranes. The lighter uranium-235 passes through slightly faster than the uranium-238 – the other uranium isotope. In order to produce fuel that contains significant levels of uranium-235, this operation must sometimes be repeated several hundred times. Enriched fuel is used in nearly all nuclear reactors and is a major part of nuclear plant costs. But, inside a reactor, some uranium-238 is also transformed into plutonium-239 when bombarded with neutrons. Plutonium-239 is an excellent fissile material and is the main ingredient of nuclear bombs today. The atom bombs which were dropped on Hiroshima and Nagasaki were made from these two different sources. The first was made of uranium-235 which was obtained by laboriously enriching natural uranium at the first, primitive separation plants. The second was made of plutonium that was manufactured inside special reactors built at Hanford in the United States.

contained to prevent loss of life. Such containment has proved to be remarkably difficult to achieve. Apart from preventing the escape of radiation itself, great care must be taken with coolant and reactor parts that become dangerously contaminated after contact with highly radioactive particles within the core.

The result is a highly complex array of safety measures. Many reactors have secondary domes placed over them. Similarly heat exchangers are built so that radioactive coolant is not used directly to run turbines. Emergency cooling systems which can instantly spray water or gas on overheating cores are also installed. As we shall see later in this chapter, such complex systems – for all their alleged infallibility – have gone dangerously wrong on a worrying number of occasions.

Such considerations were not on the minds of the world's first nuclear enthusiasts and designers, however. Their prime concern was to build bigger and better atomic weapons. The only reactors that interested them were those which could produce plutonium.

Only Canada, which had been involved with Britain and the United States in making the first atom bombs, considered the peaceful uses of nuclear energy from the start.

In 1946, aggrieved that it had been excluded from participation in international nuclear projects by an act of the US Congress which forbade US scientists from giving information on nuclear energy to foreign colleagues, Canada turned its back on building its own nuclear weapons. Instead, Canadian engineers began work on two small power reactors at Chalk River near Ottawa. One of these, the small 'NRX' reactor, became the forerunner of the Candu reactor, possibly the most successful reactor system that has been developed to date.

*

Britain, on the other hand, was determined that it would have nuclear bombs of its own. In January 1947, an ad hoc group of six government ministers headed by Prime Minister Clement Attlee met in secrecy and committed the country to a crash programme of atom bomb construction. The public, parliament, and even most of the cabinet knew nothing of this decision, for all its importance. Sixteen months elapsed before the first public mention was made – and only then, in typically British fashion, in a three-word clause in an obscure answer to a parliamentary question.

The 1947 decision triggered a furious race to build 'the British bomb'. A massive construction project began at an old munitions factory on the Cumbrian coast. The factory was to become the nucleus of the new atomic Britain of the twentieth century. The site became known as Windscale. From the beginning, operations there were dogged by an obsessive bureaucratic secrecy which confounded the extreme urgency with which the government viewed the project.

Starved of urgent supplies in austerity-afflicted post-war Britain, the project quickly began to lag alarmingly behind schedule. Eventually its leaders were forced to approach Prime Minister Attlee directly. He promptly wrote them a note giving their needs absolute priority. Sadly for the team, the note was classified 'top secret' before it left Attlee's office – which meant that officials allocating materials could not be allowed to see it – with the result that the project had to go on competing for resources.

Such a bizarre start did not augur well for Windscale. In fact, matters only worsened. Sir Christopher Hinton, the brilliant engineer in charge of the Windscale project, was actually forbidden to make any mention of the pipeline that took radioactive waste from the plant to the sea – even though it dominated the local beach and everyone knew what it was. Even more ludicrous was the fact that, throughout this period, the London newspapers were arriving every day at the local railway station – marked for delivery to 'The Atom Bomb Plant'.

Despite such peculiar hurdles, the project was spectacularly successful. By 1952, the first plutonium-producing reactor was in operation, and only two years later the first bomb was exploded. By then Britain was seriously considering using nuclear power for peaceful purposes. Using the Windscale reactors as a model, nuclear engineers planned and built a larger version designed for power generation. On 17 October 1956, the Queen ceremoniously connected the Calder Hall nuclear generator at Windscale to the national grid.

It was another historic event – for the Calder Hall reactor was the first industrial-scale nuclear reactor to produce electricity in the world. (Both the United States and the Soviet Union claim they were the first to produce nuclear electricity – but their reactors were fairly feeble, producing only 2.4 and 5 megawatts of electricity respectively. By comparison, the Calder Hall reactor – which still operates today – is a relative giant producing 50 megawatts of power.) It has the rightful claim to be the world's first real nuclear power reactor.

Today, Britain has a total of 38 working reactors and a further 4 under construction. Last year these reactors provided 19.3 per cent of the nation's electricity. The cornerstone of this extensive programme was Calder Hall. Its design is based on a huge welded steel pressure vessel that contains the reactor's graphite core. Natural uranium metal is placed inside special magnesium alloy containers which are fitted into the core. This alloy is known as Magnox and it gave its name to the whole generation of nuclear reactors that were built over the next ten years in the United Kingdom.

Magnox reactors, which use carbon dioxide as coolant,

were eventually redesigned so that each could produce 275 megawatts of electric power. They remained, however, relatively inefficient, low-powered machines and work began from early on on a second generation of UK nuclear plants, the advanced gas-cooled reactor (AGR). Based on the same graphite moderator, carbon-dioxide cooled system as the Magnox, the AGR was capable of a significant increase in electricity production – more than 600 megawatts each.

Flushed with unbridled nuclear enthusiasm the 1964–70 Labour government promptly ordered five giant twin-reactor stations, even though the country's nuclear physicists' and engineers' previous experience of AGRs had been limited to building only one small prototype. 'We have hit the jackpot this time,' claimed the Minister of Power, Mr Fred Lee. These proved to be rash words, for, in the rush to build the reactors, three different consortia of companies were set up to build three different types of AGR – a move which many believe spread the nation's nuclear expertise too thinly. On top of this, industrial disputes, management rows and design changes during construction began to plague the AGR. Long delays set in and by the early 1980s, only two of the five double reactors ordered had been built – at Hunterston in Scotland, and at Hinkley Point. At the other three stations, Heysham, Dungeness and Hartlepool, only one reactor of each planned pair had been built by that time and these have all suffered frequent operating problems. Prices also spiralled alarmingly. For instance, the construction of one AGR – at Dungeness in Kent – was expected finally to cost more than six times its original estimate of £89 million.

The AGR fiasco proved to be a turning point in British nuclear history and marked the beginning of the industry's fall from economic grace. Utterly disillusioned with the AGR, the Central Electricity Generating Board (CEGB), led by its ebullient and vociferously pro-nuclear chairman

Lord Marshall, announced its intention to turn to the American pressurized water reactor for future nuclear power generation in Britain. The British government originally committed itself to building ten PWRs, but has since scaled this plan down to the construction of five. However, the proposal to build the first of these – at Sizewell in Suffolk – has been delayed for several years while opponents and supporters have argued over its merits at the country's longest-running public inquiry. The report of that inquiry's inspector has still to be published.

Britain's nuclear woes have not been purely economic ones. Indeed, until Chernobyl spewed its toxic fumes into the upper atmosphere, her leading nuclear installation – Windscale (later renamed Sellafield for cosmetic purposes in May 1981) – had acquired the notoriety of being the world's worst for dangerous radioactive discharges. As a result of Windscale, the Irish Sea is now the most radioactive sea in the world and is likely to remain that way for a long time. The plant has discharged more than one-quarter of a tonne of plutonium which now lies at the bottom of the Irish Sea and which will remain intensely radioactive for a quarter of a million years. In 1985, the European parliament only narrowly avoided passing a motion urging the immediate closure of Windscale – a move that would have hugely embarrassed the British government.

Worse still, some of Windscale's radioactive discharges have been returning to land when sediments are washed ashore, in sea spray, and when fish and shellfish are caught. Some evidence has been discovered which indicates that cattle and sheep grazing on contaminated pastures near the reactor have accumulated levels of plutonium and caesium in their livers hundreds of times higher than normal. Local fishermen who eat their own catches receive three times as much radiation each year as is thought to be prudent under international radiation guidelines. Environmentalists also blame the discharges for nearby Seascale's leukaemia cluster.

It is clear that much of Windscale's history has been peppered with accidents and 'near misses'. In October 1976, a leak of radioactive strontium and caesium from a waste silo was found – by chance – during building work. Only then was it realized that the leak had probably existed for four years. While this problem was being investigated, another huge leak was found in an adjacent building – one that had probably been going on for even longer, perhaps for the previous seven years. Then, in 1983, a large quantity of radioactive solvents was released into the North Sea. Ministers were not informed for a week and the environment minister, William Waldegrave, said that but for chance he might never have been informed about the accident. Gross managerial incompetence was revealed during the ensuing investigation and British Nuclear Fuels was prosecuted, found guilty on four charges and fined £10,000 with £60,000 costs.

In all, there have been more than 300 accidents, both large and small, at Windscale and the plant has come under strong criticism from parties both inside and outside the nuclear industry. However, none of these incidents reached the dimensions of the events which began on the morning of 8 October 1957, when a physicist in charge of Windscale's Number One plutonium production reactor made a critical error. He threw a switch too soon while carrying out a routine operation. He had no operating manual to help him and vital instruments were in the wrong position to give him accurate measurements. The result was fire which rapidly engulfed the reactor and blazed out of control for 42 hours, with no one at the plant even aware that disaster was imminent. By the time the alarm was raised, uranium fuel cladding and graphite were all on fire. Mr Ronald Gausden, the manager of the plant, removed a plug in a wall of the reactor and 'looked the monster in the eye'. He recalls: 'It wasn't a meltdown but I knew I was looking at the start of one.'

First, the staff sprayed the fire with carbon dioxide, but this proved to be useless. Then, like the emergency teams later did at Chernobyl, they considered using water – aware that it might lead to an explosion that would blast the reactor apart. For a further day the fire continued to blaze out of control. Britain was on the brink of nuclear catastrophe. At 8.55 a.m. on Friday, 11 October, panic-struck nuclear chiefs decided to take the risk and use 'a tidal wave' of water. The gamble paid off. By 3.10 p.m. the following day, the fire had been extinguished.

Only later was it realized how narrowly was a full-scale disaster avoided – by the installation of filters which trapped most of the deadly radioactive isotopes thrown in the air by the fire. Yet these filters were very nearly rejected from the reactor's plans. They had only been installed at the insistence of Sir John Cockcroft, one of the fathers of the British atomic bomb project, as a precautionary measure. At the time, most of his colleagues thought their construction ridiculous. The filters were dubbed 'Cockcroft's Folly' and at one point the Windscale management even considered removing them to save money. Had they done so, there would have been considerably more fall-out and a greater disaster would have struck the country.

As it was, a considerable discharge of radioactive material did occur – though British people were misled about the danger. Britons were not told of the fire until it had almost been extinguished and much of what they were told was untrue. Those government ministers and nuclear chiefs who so quickly chastised the Russians for their secrecy over the Chernobyl fire seem to have forgotten how their own predecessors behaved.

Just as with Chernobyl, official reaction was slow in the

extreme. There was no evacuation of houses near the plant. Not until Saturday evening, after the fire had been extinguished, were local milk sales banned – and then only from a 14-square-mile area round Windscale. By the Monday, the ban had to be extended to a 500-square-mile area and, in all, a total of 2 million litres of milk destroyed. As one woman pointed out in a letter to the local *Whitehaven News*:

We were given no warning until the situation was under control. Why not? Suppose the situation had 'run away'? What then? Surely people have a right to be given enough warning either to move their children out of the vicinity, or at least to keep them indoors if any severe accident is expected.

After the debris had been cleaned up, the burnt-out reactor was entombed in concrete. Its highly radioactive remains have lain undisturbed at Windscale for the past two decades – as will the remains of the far more massive Chernobyl reactor which is also to be entombed in concrete. Both are monuments to the fallibility of the world's nuclear industry.

An inquiry was held into the Windscale blaze, but the resulting report was never published in its full form. The expurgated version published soon afterwards did admit that high levels of radioactive escapes did occur though it was to 'the highest degree unlikely that any harm was done to the health of anybody'. Such assurances have not stood the test of time. In 1983, the National Radiological Protection Board, prompted by the independent calculations of an environmental research group, produced a report which admitted that about 260 people are likely to have contracted thyroid cancer as a result of the Windscale fire's discharges. Thirty-three people will have died of cancer or sustained genetic damage that will bring disease or death to their descendants.

*

This litany of nuclear horrors was not restricted only to the British civil programme. British atom bomb projects have been similarly bedevilled by blunders and cynical indifference to innocent individuals. The UK atom bomb programme involved a series of test explosions which were carried out in Australia and the small colonial islands of the Pacific. They subsequently triggered enormous resentment despite attempts to impose military secrecy and suppress the facts that among the 20,000 British servicemen, Australian soldiers and pilots, and Aborigines on the sites, many were contaminated; and that uncleared plutonium debris was left in the desert.

In 1953, Britain exploded a relatively small (12 kiloton) bomb, code-named Totem 1, in a hastily prepared desert site at Emu. The choice of this site was imposed on the British military because their previous island site at Monte Bello had become too contaminated for re-use. Totem 1 had all the elements of rush, secrecy, negligence and over-optimism that characterized the atom bomb tests of the period. In this case, the test was carried out to discover if plutonium from civil reactors could be used to make atom bombs. Plutonium made in Magnox reactors is not ideal for bomb making. It is contaminated with the isotope plutonium-240, which does not support fission as well as plutonium-239. However, if the Totem test showed that plutonium-240 could be used as a significant atom bomb component, it would 'lead to economies in the long run', the British defence minister Earl Alexander was briefed in a very short top secret paper. Behind the test lay the warning of Churchill's scientific adviser Lord Cherwell that a British rejection of nuclear power would be 'national suicide'.

The Totem test worked. But it also sent a cigar-shaped cloud drifting 150 kilometres north over an Aborigine encampment because the bomb had been exploded in unsuitable weather conditions. The Aborigines experienced vomiting and blindness and some were exposed to up to 80 rems of radiation from the terrifying 'black mist' that enveloped them. In addition, bomber pilots were required to fly through the radioactive cloud to carry out measurements for scientists on the ground. Unfortunately, the cloud was much 'hotter' than anticipated and the planes were contaminated and left unusable. Monitoring instruments also proved to be inadequate. Some pilots and mechanics were exposed to up to 50 rems of radiation which led Air Vice Marshal Daley of the Australian air force to write angrily to the British government: 'We were firmly told this was not a hazard. Now it appears that there was a hazard.'

In other episodes during the military programme, servicemen were gathered in the open air less than 8 kilometres from a small blast to 'indoctrinate' them, that is to accustom them to manoeuvres during an atomic war. Others were placed in tanks closer than 1,000 metres. Ships were ordered to sail through radioactive clouds, or were doused with radioactive dust to see if it could be hosed away.

No follow-up health studies were ever conducted on contaminated individuals and military secrecy prevented any analysis of the risks that were taken at a time when radioactive hazards were poorly understood. It was only in the 1980s that British and Australian servicemen began to assemble data on the cancers, birth defects and cataracts which began to affect themselves and their families. Eventually, an Australian defence minister openly accused the British government of having been 'incompetent – if not downright careless'.

Britain has not been alone in facing severe problems in developing both civil and military nuclear programmes. The question of who should control the power of the atom as it emerged from its début at Hiroshima and Nagasaki was no more hotly contested than in the United States, where military leaders were demanding bigger and bigger bombs and industrialists were slavering over the endlessly enticing illusion of cheap energy. The military sought the atom. So did industry. At first the United States congress intervened by creating a new government institution, the United States Atomic Energy Commission, with a mandate to conserve and restrict 'the use of atomic energy for the national defense, to prohibit its private exploitation and preserve the secret and confidential character of information concerning the use and application of atomic energy'. American scientists, including Robert Oppenheimer, the director of the Los Alamos bomb factory, played down the possibility of nuclear power and concentrated on building weapons. The emphasis on the security of America came directly from the President. Harry Truman considered the power of the atom 'too important to be made the subject of profit seeking'. But, all that changed with the arrival in the White House of his successor, Dwight Eisenhower, who was more finely tuned to the needs and wishes of the business community. Eisenhower appointed a pugnacious Wall Street banker, Lewis Strauss, to head the AEC and Strauss began to promote civilian nuclear power. In his famous 'atoms for peace' speech in 1953, the president codified the new US approach. 'It is not enough', he said, 'to take this weapon out the hands of soldiers. It must be put into the hands of those who will know how to strip its military casing and adapt it to the art of peace.'

In a frenzy of public-relations activity following the speech, the US government produced a pamphlet containing Eisenhower's remarks in ten languages and, two weeks after delivery, over 200,000 copies had been sent out by American firms in their foreign mail; 350 US foreign-language newspapers and related ethnic organizations started a campaign to ensure that excerpts of the speech were sent by immigrants to their relatives and friends abroad. The sphere of the so-called peaceful atom expanded rapidly as the Voice of America radio broadcast talks to the world with titles like, 'Nuclear Device in Fight Against Cancer'; 'Forestry Experts Predict Atomic Rays will Cut Lumber Instead of Saws', and 'Atomic Locomotive Designed'.

In congress the Democrats moved to prevent atomic energy from being given away to greedy big business, arguing that the AEC could build and operate reactors for the benefit of all. But big business won. The 1954 Atomic Energy Act encouraged private corporations to move into the new wonderland. Ironically, the man who dominated the start of commercial nuclear development in the United States was not a businessman but a Navy captain, Hyman Rickover. He saw early on the potential of a submarine that never had to go into port to refuel: and by hard work, dedication and a lot of ingenuity he delivered the world's first nuclear-powered submarine for the US Navy in January 1955. The AEC, delighted at his success, grabbed his reactor, a pressurized water-cooled type, for a joint project with the manufacturers Westinghouse and the first American electric utility to 'go nuclear', the Duquesne Light Company of Pittsburgh. In the ground-breaking ceremony, Eisenhower waved a magic electronic wand over the site on the Ohio River to start the first bulldozer.

Still, the other US utility executives were reluctant to join up. They remained unconvinced that the higher construction costs of the reactors − even the government was saying the nuclear plants would cost 60 per cent more than conventional plants − would be a good investment, they were wary that the plants would not be reliable, that supplies of uranium fuel might be hard to come by, and that insurance companies would be worried about the potential hazards and decline full insurance. Charles Weaver, the engineer-turned salesman vice-president of Westinghouse, observed, 'We cannot exclude the possibility that a great enough fool aided by a great enough conspiracy of circumstances could bring about an accident exceeding the available insurance.' The government, in an effort to calm such concerns, commissioned a report on a 'worst-case' accident, but it did more harm than good to the government's cause. (See Chapter 2 for a discussion of this episode.)

The government's rush to promote nuclear power meant that it sidestepped major considerations of safety, brushing aside those who suggested that a slower lane might, in the end, be more prudent. The nuclear zealots had the backing of the President. Eisenhower launched a massive subsidy for an internal market in US reactors with his 'atoms for peace' programme, in effect, subsidizing what was to become a short-term lucrative market for America's two electrical giants, Westinghouse and General Electric.

By 1962 the AEC had spent 1·3 billion dollars promoting nuclear power – more than twice the investment made by private companies. Still, the utilities remained conservative, refusing to rise to the bait, so the manufacturers decided to make them an offer they could not refuse – a package deal of a completed reactor for a set price, with no extra payment for construction delays, strikes, material shortages and the like. In 1963, General Electric sold the first so-called 'turnkey' contract to the Jersey Central Light and Power Company for a reactor at Oyster Creek. The reactor passed into folklore as the first 'commercial plant'. The new fixed-price contracts, hopelessly underpriced by the manufacturers, lost an average of 75 million dollars on each deal. But the utilities jumped on the 'great nuclear bandwagon' and reactor orders soared from 7 in 1965 to 30 two years later. The gamble was enormous, however. No engineer was certain how the bigger and bigger reactors being ordered would turn out; or what extra costs would have to be included to take care of the more complicated 'plumbing'. In the end, for the makers, the dream turned into a nightmare of cost overruns and demands for stricter regulations of safety and environmental protection. On top of this came an economic downturn that reduced the average increase in electrical consumption from a magical 7 per cent a year during the 1960s to zero by the late 1970s.

Then, suddenly, nuclear engineers started to leave the industry, claiming the plants were unsafe. Concerned citizens were turned off nuclear power as rapidly and as effectively as Westinghouse and General Electric had turned on the utility companies in the first place. It was not really suprising, for the public had never really believed official assurances enshrined in the 1975 Rasmussen Report (and endorsed in Britain by Lord Marshall as Chairman of the Central Electricity Generating Board), that a Chernobyl-style accident could only happen once in a million years of a reactor's operation.

Indeed, there was plenty of evidence that a serious accident was just waiting to happen. In 1982 an American government study showed that there had been 169 incidents that could have led to a meltdown in the United States between 1969 and 1979 alone. There were some desperately close shaves. On 5 October 1966, part of the nuclear fuel melted in the core of the Enrico-Fermi 1 experimental fast breeder reactor outside Detroit. No one knew what to do. Fortunately, the accident stopped short of disaster. A relieved engineer from the firm that built the reactor commented, 'We almost lost Detroit.' On 22 March 1975, an electrician and his mate lit a candle to try to detect a draught among the cables beneath the control room of the Browns Ferry power station in Alabama, newly inaugurated as the biggest in the world. The cables caught fire, and in the resulting seven-hour conflagration all five of the emergency cooling systems on one reactor – needed to prevent a meltdown – were knocked out. A major catastrophe was only narrowly averted. Later it emerged that officials had issued a formal warning of the 'probability of a catastrophic fire' at Browns Ferry – but that it had been ignored.

The most famous American accident of all took place just two weeks after the release of the anti-nuclear film *The China Syndrome*, starring Jane Fonda and Jack Lemmon. When the film came out, it was immediately attacked by the nuclear industry and conservative commentators for depicting an impossible situation. Yet on 28 March 1979, a whole series of failures and operator mistakes turned a routine equipment malfunction at Three Mile Island, near Harrisburg, Pennsylvania into a drama that mirrored many of the scenes of *The China Syndrome*. It is thought that the reactor came within an hour of a full meltdown.

As the accident progressed it became clear that no one had any idea what to do. On the Friday Mr Joseph M. Hendrie, Chairman of the government's Nuclear Regulatory Commission (NRC), which held a continuous five-day meeting to try to control the situation, told his colleagues, 'We are operating almost totally in the blind. The governor's information is ambiguous, mine is nonexistent and – I don't know – it's like a couple of blind men staggering around making decisions.'

Like the UK Windscale fire, the Three Mile Island incident reflects no credit on a government and nuclear industry that was soon to criticize the Soviet Union over Chernobyl for misinformation and tardiness in evacuating local people. As *Time* magazine commented at the time: 'Reassuring statements spewed from the plant's press spokesmen, sounding as if they were taken right out of the script for *The China Syndrome*.' And the authorities' approach to evacuation was even more alarming. On the Friday, two days after the start of the accident, one of the NRC's most senior officials, Harold Denton, told the commissioners that they should start evacuating people before a serious escape of radioactivity took place 'rather than sitting here waiting to die'. Yet a day later they had still not done it. Another top official, Roger Mattson, then drove the point home:

We have got an accident that we have never been designed to accommodate and it is, in the best estimate, deteriorating slowly and, on the most pessimistic estimate it is on the threshold of turning bad. I do not have a reason for not moving people. I don't know what you are protecting by not moving people.

The commissioners still decided against recommending evacuation.

The official Kemeny commission set up by President Carter to investigate the accident concluded that complacency had so pervaded the industry that 'we are convinced that an accident like Three Mile Island was eventually inevitable.' It judged that a meltdown had only been avoided through sheer luck.

The American accidents show that human frailty can overwhelm the most 'fail-safe' safety systems, and that once an accident begins people tend to panic. One leading reactor safety engineer put it like this:

Plants grow more complex. Safety hangs increasingly on the human error factor, and we can't eliminate it. Most of our operators have seen emergencies only on a simulator. The real thing can look quite different, and they may have just 60 terrified seconds to act.

Or, as one witness of Three Mile Island put it: 'Bells were ringing, lights were flashing, and everyone was grabbing and scratching.'

One senior NRC official, Dr Stephen Hanauer, collected a secret file – 30 cm (12 in.) thick – on horror stories from the nuclear industry. The file, eventually made public through the Freedom of Information Act, makes horrific reading. At one nuclear reactor 'a regulation basketball' wrapped in rubber tape was used to plug a pipe. Inevitably water pressure shot it out like a bullet from a gun, and 14,000 gallons of radioactive water escaped. At another reactor, a 3,000 gallon radioactive waste tank was connected to a drinking fountain. Official investigators concluded that 'in general' this was considered 'poor practice'. The file recounts how safety systems have been disabled when valves and switches have been left in the wrong position, sometimes for weeks on end, how important safety equipment has been installed backwards or upside down and how an entire welding rig was left inside a reactor, blocking important water flows. It tells of safety tests that were not carried out, ones that failed to detect faults, and incidents where operators decided to go on running their reactors even after safety equipment was shown to be faulty, or ignored warning signals because they had lost confidence in the reliability of their instruments.

The development of nuclear energy in Britain and the United States has clearly been an unhappy process – as many in the industry now ruefully admit. For their part, they turn enviously to Europe, and in particular to France which is held by them to be a model of sensible planning and engineering. Certainly French nuclear power generation has been massively successful as a civil engineering exercise. While Britain wandered chaotically from one gas-cooled reactor design to another, France – which has little coal or oil of its own – confidently plumped for a single design, based on US Westinghouse plans, and used it as a basic model for reactor construction round the country.

With typical Gallic centralism, a massive reactor construction programme was ruthlessly imposed by government. As a result, between 1975 and 1985, a total of 33 PWR plants were built and a further 22 will be constructed by 1990. It is an astonishing commitment which will allow France to generate three-quarters of its power from nuclear generators.

The programme has been carried out with commendable efficiency and zeal – though not without an adverse impact on civil liberties. To prevent the delays which have blighted the nuclear aspirations of countries such as Britain, the French simply by-passed public inquiries which should have been held into reactor construction plans. As the director of the French electricity board Electricité de France (EdF) M. Remy Carle, candidly puts it: 'You don't tell the frogs when you are draining the marsh.' Sir Frederick Warner, the distinguished UK radiologist, is equally blunt. In the *Guardian*, he recalled the demonstration which took place at the Flamanville reactor in France: 'The French called out the riot police. One demonstrator was killed. The exercise cost £200,000 whereas we spent £3 million on the Windscale inquiry. It seems the French spent their money more effectively.'

The imposition of nuclear power on such a gargantuan scale has also brought massive economic problems to France. Forced to raise cash for the programme on international money markets, the EdF has been driven into enormous debt. Today, it owes $200 billion and is now one of biggest debtors in the world. In a bid to pay off these debts, EdF chiefs have been forced to scurry round Europe to sell the country's massive excess of power – with only partial success.

The French have also come in for widespread criticism as they insist on continuing with nuclear bomb tests. Their tests at the Mururoa atoll in French Polynesia have been particularly controversial. Since 1973, a series of underground bomb explosions have been carried out at the coral atoll. French scientists claim these are perfectly safe because molten rock effectively seals in the radioactive inventories left after the explosions. But, at least two major accidents have occurred at Mururoa. In 1979, an underground test went badly wrong, triggering a tidal wave and an earthquake. In a separate incident, an underground laboratory, used for experiments on plutonium, caught fire, leading to an explosion that killed two workers. The blast also caused widespread land and sea contamination. Today, the atoll – which has been the site of more than 80 nuclear bomb explosions – is slowly fracturing 'like a Swiss cheese', say French critics of their country's nuclear programme. France conceals radiation readings and health statistics in the former paradise around Tahiti.

French methods for dealing with protesters have also caused controversy. In 1973, they began ramming boats and beating up crews of protest groups such as Greenpeace (who nevertheless forced the French government to carry out future tests underground). Then, in 1985, agents of the French secret service blew up a Greenpeace boat in a New Zealand harbour, killing one man and creating a bitter international incident.

Nuclear problems have not only been the province of the western 'Great Powers'. Japan, which has one of the largest nuclear development programmes in the world today, has suffered considerable embarrassment from nuclear breakdowns. In 1974, for example, the Japanese nuclear ship development agency launched its prototype nuclear-powered cargo ship, the *Mutsu*. Its career was inglorious. Local fishermen delayed its launch for two years. Even when a 100 million yen compensation fund was set up, 250 small boats still attempted to blockade the *Mutsu* in harbour.

Eventually, the *Mutsu* slipped out to sea during a typhoon. Its reactor promptly developed a radiation leak during its start-up. The crew, fearful of returning to land with the ship in such a condition, attempted to plug the leak, first with a concoction that consisted mainly of boiled rice, and then with their old socks. The crippled ship drifted for 45 days before finally being allowed to return to harbour.

Despite such incidents, Japan's nuclear power programme has grown because of national fears of energy shortages. Japan imports the bulk of its energy, to supply 117 million people squeezed in a small country. Its government intended – before Chernobyl – to supply half the country's power needs from nuclear plants by the end of the century. This would involve a six-fold expansion of the current Japanese complement of 25 nuclear plants. But these plans have had to face growing political opposition as fears about nuclear plant safety have mounted. There has been at least one accidental release of radioactivity from a Japanese plant. As reactors are all, inevitably, built near population centres, fisheries or beaches, the dangers facing the country are keenly felt. Japan also faces frequent earthquakes – which could severely damage nuclear plants – and a difficult problem of waste disposal. Attempts to hire British facilities to dispose of waste have also run into hostility in the UK.

In West Germany, a vigorous nuclear power programme has steadily run into the slow-downs and uncertainties which have been common problems for many other western nations. Public opposition has been particularly vociferous, with one mass demonstration near Hamburg in 1981 needing the biggest police response in the republic's short history.

Licensing hearings and court actions by environmentalists

have also had an impact. Only one new nuclear power station has been ordered since 1975.

In Sweden, a 1980 referendum voted to halt the country's considerable commitment to nuclear power. A total of nine complete plants and two partially completed ones are to be phased out by 2010, even though they currently provide more than 30 per cent of Sweden's electricity.

Austria's only reactor, at Zwentendorf, faces a similar fate. The plant was completed in 1978, but has never been commissioned because a referendum in the same year decided against commissioning it. The plant has lain idle since then.

Australia has refused to build any nuclear plants. And so has Denmark – although the country's safety is still threatned by nearby Swedish plants on the Baltic close to Denmark.

Western nations have not confined their nuclear aspirations to within their own borders. Several have also embarked on disturbing export drives to sell their reactors to the Third World. Large reactors are unsuitable for the smallest, poorest countries. A single reactor that supplies more than 15 per cent of a country's needs causes mayhem to its national grid if forced to shut down.

Nevertheless, developing nations such as India, Brazil, Mexico, the Philippines, Pakistan, South Africa, South Korea and Taiwan have begun nuclear programmes. Of these, India has the largest. It has six reactors in operation and a further eight are under construction or in planning. India also has an appalling nuclear safety record. Its Tarapur nuclear reactor in Maharashtra is reported to have broken several world records for radioactive pollution and has exposed more than 300 men to doses above international limits. In the first 11 years of Tarapur's operation, it suffered 344 'unusual occurrences' – the euphemism for failures, emergencies and accidents. In 1980, it is reported that the plant came close to a meltdown. Parts of the power station, supposedly accessible to workers, are so 'hot' with radiation that anyone entering them would get a fatal dose in a matter of minutes.

Other Indian reactors have equally bad reputations. For instance, the Kota power station in Rajastan is considered to be the world's second most polluted station after Tarapur while one of the country's planned reactors, at Norora, in Uttar Pradesh, will be built in an earthquake-prone region.

Meanwhile, 4,000 deficiencies have been found in a planned reactor in the Philippines by inspectors from the International Atomic Energy Agency.

Nuclear reactors in Third World countries also face a special danger. Poverty often means political instability. This is something nuclear power can scarcely afford. A nuclear reactor, with its menacing contents, is a prime target for hostile military, or terrorist action.

Even if environmentalists could have their way today, it is certain that the headaches brought by nuclear power will not quickly disappear. For a start, something must be done about nuclear waste – some of which will remain intensely dangerous for hundreds of thousands of years. No one knows how to keep it isolated from all living things for anything like that length of time – and many governments are having extreme difficulty persuading their peoples to agree to the disposal even of low-level short-lived radioactive waste. Then, as the Worldwatch Institute reported in April 1986, the vexing problem of how to dismantle old nuclear reactors has scarcely received any attention, although many plants are nearing the ends of their working lives. 'Not one of the 26 countries currently relying on nuclear power is adequately prepared for this undertaking,' says the report.

In all, this story is a depressing one. In crucial ways, it is little more than a catalogue of human error, complacency and wilful indifference to danger. Forty years ago, nuclear energy was the great white hope of the twentieth century. Today, the western nuclear industry is a thoroughly demoralized conglomerate of uneasy nations and companies. It was not in the west, however, that the dream of nuclear power was to receive its most catastrophic global blow. Nuclear energy was just as much a post-war preoccupation with the Soviet Union as with any of its western rivals. But there, history took a very different – and even more disaster-prone – course.

4 The Red Specialists

'Communism is Soviet power plus the electrification of the whole country.'

V. I. Lenin

A few months after America's worst nuclear power accident at Three Mile Island in 1979, Dick Thornborough, the governor of Pennsylvania, visited the Soviet Union. The governor wondered if the alarming accident, which had resulted in a popular demand for reform of US nuclear safety standards, would have any effect on the burgeoning Soviet nuclear power programme. One Soviet official, Dzherman M. Gvisiani, then deputy chairman of the Soviet Committee for Science and Technology, told Thornborough bluntly: 'Safety is a solved problem in the Soviet Union.' No similar accidents had occurred, he said, and the problems raised at Three Mile Island had been 'over-dramatized'. For Thornborough, who had been at the centre of the public outcry against the US reactor manufacturers, Gvisiani's confident assertion was reminiscent of a bygone age in nuclear power in the United States when, as he put it: 'We used to hear the same thing from industry and regulatory officials.'

Before Chernobyl, certainly, there were no more eager and devoted disciples of making electricity from the atom than the builders of Soviet nuclear power. Indeed, a list of their achievements was sometimes wistfully admired by western nuclear officials as evidence that nuclear power was both safe and a viable form of energy. The dedication of the Soviet nuclear establishment had, indeed, been admirable.

Soviet scientists and engineers had overcome the terrible devastation and economic deprivation the country had suffered during the Second World War and, in 1949, had produced enough plutonium from a reactor to make an atomic bomb. In 1954, they built the world's first small nuclear reactor to provide electrical power to a community and, today, unlike America, where no nuclear plants have been ordered for a decade, the Soviet Union has the largest nuclear construction programme in the world. The power of the atom gave Soviet scientists an opportunity – one of the best they had ever had – to proclaim a progressive vision for the future and relish a sense of achievement for the Soviet state. In particular, nuclear power gave the Soviets a chance to develop an advanced indigenous industry that would have obvious positive benefits as a source of modernization throughout the whole economy.

Because the Americans had built a bomb first, the Soviets considered their own bomb a military priority, but making electricity from nuclear power appealed to them as much, if not more, than to the capitalist enterprises which had exploited nuclear power in the west. The handpicked Soviet scientists and engineers set about their task with determination and patriotic enthusiasm equalling, if not surpassing, that of their counterparts in the American wartime Manhattan Project that produced the world's first atomic weapons. Although many leading Russian scientists had been victims of the purges of the 1930s, there was no question of refusing to make a bomb for Stalin – the shock of the German invasion had, for most, overcome hostility toward and fear of the Stalin regime. Nor was there any lack of expertise. Soviet scientists had been keenly aware of the major advances in atomic physics – including the knowledge that a chain reaction using uranium was possible – that had coincided with the start of the Second World War. They had completed important nuclear experiments of their own and, in 1942, had begun a fledgling nuclear programme.

However, because a Soviet bomb was a priority, the Soviet nuclear power programme had lagged somewhat behind the west's. As America and Britain prepared themselves, in the late 1950s, for massive promotion campaigns to capture the emerging nuclear reactor export market, the Soviets were still concerned with producing enough plutonium for the weapons projects. But, like their western rivals, they were also busy designing a wide range of reactor types, including the controversial breeder reactor. The Soviet scientists were surprisingly open about their frustrations on the few occasions they were allowed to come to the west. In 1955, at the first of the international conferences in Geneva on the so-called 'peaceful atom', the head of the US delegation, the physicist Isidor Rabi, commented, 'Right now I would say that the old iron curtain is composed of almost equal parts of iron and red tape. Of the two, the red tape is the harder to figure.'

But the Soviet system had its advantages for the Soviet nuclear establishment. When their western counterparts had to cope with the effects of an economic recession in the mid-1970s, they surged ahead with nuclear power programmes that included reactors half as big again as the ones which were being cancelled by reluctant, and, in some cases, disillusioned, electrical utilities in America. The CIA concluded in a 1985 Soviet assessment that:

based on the aggressive programme the Soviet Union now has on the books to expand existing plants and add new ones, most informed observers expect that growth should continue throughout this decade and into the early 1990s, even with continuing construction bottlenecks.

The overtly political decision-making of the Soviet economy, in which the criteria of cost and price, supply and demand play only a partial role, permitted huge plans for the expansion of nuclear power. It also satisfied the Soviet concept of what some western economists refer to as 'giantism', a particular characteristic of Soviet planning that is fired by widespread technological optimism. And in a society riddled with restrictions like the Soviet society, it was also possible to build nuclear power plants to a minimum standard of safety. The Soviet nuclear planners never had to produce such a typically American planning phenomenon as an 'environmental impact statement', nor submit their blueprints to a royal commission or some such institutional process of western democracies. There is no governmental or independent watchdog standing over the decisions of central government in Moscow. Major Soviet decisions on economic priorities are taken by a comparatively small group of people at the highest levels in the Party and state apparatus, a process that allows little opportunity for dissenters. Additional costs are not forced on the Soviet planners from environmental groups similar to the ones in the United States. In America, such groups are estimated to have increased the cost of a typical 1,000 megawatt nuclear power plant by more than $100,000,000. Finally, until the accident at Chernobyl, there was little evidence that Soviet citizens were concerned about the potential hazards of nuclear power. They appeared, like most Soviet scientists and engineers, to consider its ascendancy in Soviet energy production as a measure of the country's progress and a matter of national pride. This might have been as much a function of the ignorance of the potential hazards and of the nuclear accidents that are known by westerners to have occurred in the Soviet Union, as it was an institutional desire to be good disciples of Lenin's ideology about power and electricity.

Before Chernobyl, the benefits rather than the deficiencies and potential harmful effects of nuclear power were stressed by most Soviet scientists and engineers without significant opposition. Also, for the sake of simplicity and in the absence of reliable information, nuclear accidents in the west could always be, and mostly were, ascribed by Soviet officials to the evils of the profit motive: greedy American companies building power plants larger than known technology could handle safely, or – even simpler – the run-of-the-mill banditry of capitalist competition. After Three Mile Island, one Soviet commentator claimed that the accident had been blown out of all proportion by the US oil companies trying to smear the name of a rival technology.

The profit motive, congenial collegiate campus life and the capitalist dream of 'electricity too cheap to meter' that pervaded the early, heady days of the American nuclear power production, were not important dynamics propelling the Soviet men – no women are mentioned – who devoted their lives, and in the case of the slave labour used to build the plants, sacrificed their lives, for Soviet nuclear power. Unlike their American counterparts who worked at the Los Alamos Nuclear Weapons Laboratory in the constantly pleasing climate and among the breathtaking mesas of New Mexico, the workers on the Soviet bomb project toiled in some of the most bleak of Soviet environments. In the midst of the terrible conditions the leaders of the project adopted the trappings of full bureaucratic power – which they knew could be theirs if only they could succeed in their mission. One of two key engineer-administrators of the bomb project, Avraami Zavenyagin, impressed the handful of German scientists who also worked on the project by his sartorial elegance, always clean-shaven and dressed in an immaculate business suit. Indeed, the Soviet nuclear engineers, such as Zavenyagin, were members of a special breed of Soviet society, dubbed by western observers, the 'Red Specialists'.

They came from a distinct caste, one that had permeated the central decision-making of Soviet politics as completely as lawyers invade the process in America. Their breed is one of the most enduring legacies of the Stalin era – and one that survives even today. Most of the top leaders are engineers by training; even Gorbachev, who has a law degree, took another by correspondence in Agricultural Science. This technological elite, created intentionally by government policy in the 1920s and 1930s was chosen, as a loyal party membership, to attend courses in a series of newly established technical colleges, from which each emerged as a plant director in heavy industry. Unquestioning acceptance of the official Party ideology and the actions of the Party dominated the lives of this new cadre. From their early membership through their participation in the civil war, their technical training and their work assignments, they were exceptionally conscious of their unique role. One of the Soviet nuclear administrators, Vassily Emelyanov, recalled, 'We were the country's only hope, everything depended on us.'

The ideology of the Red Specialists was explicitly material: production was the ultimate value. They glorified large-scale construction products and believed passionately in the primacy of heavy industry. Their strongest belief opposed a centuries-old Russian cultural tradition of caution and humility in man's relationship with the power of nature. They were most definitely 'progressive'. Their job was to conquer nature, especially the more forbidding challenges of the Russian environment. Throughout the 1930s this group shared a spirit of optimism as they built dams, roads, railways lines and factories in the most inhospitable outposts of their country. In the 1940s the ultimate challenge was mastering the challenge of the atom.

When the Soviets exploded their first atomic bomb – in 1949 – many western analysts, who were reluctant to admit to Soviet atomic expertise, were quick to suggest that it was due to the wide network of Soviet atomic spies. They thought, especially, that the German refugee scientist, Klaus Fuchs, who had preyed on the American Manhattan Project, must have accounted for the Soviet success. In fact, the value of the spy ring to the Soviets remains hazy and the subject of much cold war speculation.

The chief Russian scientist on the project was Igor Kurchatov, who was relatively unknown in the west at the time but who became the only member of the bomb team to have an official biography. A tall, broad-shouldered man with a long, wispy beard, photographs of him abound in the official accounts of the Soviet nuclear programme. In 1942 he was taken off war work in Kazan, 800 kilometres to the east of Moscow and a safe distance from the invading Germans, to set up the innocuously named 'Laboratory No. 2 of the Academy of Sciences, USSR' on the outskirts of Moscow. By the end of the 1940s, a small town had grown up around the laboratory and it was given a new, equally uninformative title: 'The Laboratory for Measuring Instruments'. Not until the mid-1950s, when its most secret work had been completed, was it given its real name, 'The Institute for Atomic Energy'.

Kurchatov worked directly under Zavenyagin and another Red Specialist, Boris Vannikov, who was the nominal head of the project. Overall political direction came from Lavrenti Beria, the head of the secret police, the NKVD. Zavenyagin was Beria's man. He had been a deputy minister of Beria's own department, the Ministry of Internal Affairs, before joining the bomb project and his commitment to the state was passionate. When Zavenyagin had enrolled as a student in the Mining Institute in Moscow in the early 1930s, he was required to fill in a questionnaire about his attitude to Soviet power. 'I believe in it', or 'I support it' were the common answers. But Zavenyagin is said to have replied, 'I am ready to die for it.'

At the end of 1946 the bomb team had successfully operated their first experimental reactor at Kurchatov's laboratory. According to some western reports, the dimensions of this first reactor were almost identical to those of the fourth reactor built by the Americans at the Hanford nuclear site in Washington State, yet the Americans did not publish their Hanford design until 1953. To some, this reinforced the idea that the Soviet espionage ring in the west was, indeed, very successful, but it was still speculation.

The plutonium-producing reactors, smaller versions of the Chernobyl-type reactors to come, were built at Kyshtym in the Chelyabinsk region on the east side of the Urals. The region had been a centre of the Russian armaments industry since the time of Peter the Great, but now its residents were evacuated to make room for forced labour workers, arranged by Beria. According to western sources, it was here that the first of the so-called atomgrads were built – plants that produced all necessary materials for the Soviet nuclear weapons arsenal. The reactors were fuelled by natural uranium and moderated by graphite, the same type used to produce plutonium for the American and British bombs. The complex became known as Chelyabinsk-40, or as the CIA later codenamed it, Post Box 40. Sergei Polikanov, a Soviet scientist who once worked in Kyshtym and is now living in the west, called the complex a 'plutonium factory'.

According to Alexander Solzhenitsyn in *The Gulag Archipelago*, when the labourers had finished their work, in 1948, they were 'declared to be a particularly dangerous contingent' because of their knowledge of the secret plant. When they had served their sentences they were not allowed to go home but were transferred to camps on the Kolyma river in the far north-east of Siberia. In 1950 the CIA estimated that the Soviets had two 250-megawatt graphite moderated piles in operation producing plutonium for bombs. A third was added in 1952.

The death of Stalin, in March 1953, and the subsequent fall of his police chief Beria appears to have coincided with the rise of another Red Specialist, Vyacheslav Alexandrovich Malyshev, as the new head of the Soviet nuclear power programme. His activities are so obscured by Soviet secrecy that an official biographical sketch of him appeared without ever mentioning his nuclear role. Soviet citizens were given their first glimpse of Malyshev's new-found importance when he made a surprise appearance with members of the Soviet Politburo at the Moscow Opera in June 1953. The one missing member that night was Malyshev's predecessor, Beria, who was arrested at the theatre, later executed and his vast secret police empire dismembered.

Malyshev was no newcomer to Lenin's goal of the electrification of Russia. He had shared the dream long ago. About 80 per cent of the Soviet Union's natural energy resources are concentrated in the eastern regions of the country while 80 per cent of the population and consumers of power are in the west. An important part of Lenin's dream was to electrify the east and get people to live there, too. As a young engineer in 1931, Malyshev had given an impassioned speech to his superiors on the prospects of the hydroelectric development of Siberia. 'We shall induce 4 or 5 million people from the European sector to pack up and move to Angara, where we shall build world centres of a new communist industry,' he declared. 'The myriad lights from the east will attract hosts of young men and women like magnets. We shall bring wonderful cities into being there.' He was a clear choice to put Lenin's ideology into action. Nuclear power gave him the opportunity.

In 1954, a major new construction programme for nuclear power was launched under a new cover, the Ministry of

Medium Machine Building, with Malyshev in charge. The same year the Soviets achieved a public relations triumph in nuclear power by feeding electricity from a small 5,000-kilowatt reactor to the homes of the citizens of Obninsk, a town 100 kilometres south-west of Moscow. Soon Malyshev's ministry would be expanded to contain a new department known as the Central Directorate for the Utilization of Atomic Energy.

As the world of the atom became fully enshrined in new institutions in four other countries, the United States, Britain and Canada, the Soviets were determined not to be left behind. At the Geneva Atoms For Peace conference in 1955, mounds of scientific papers covering the whole range of the peaceful atom – from producing electricity to sterilizing sewage – titillated the imagination of the world. For their part Soviet scientists presented some of the most optimistic cost projections. They talked of building 50-megawatt reactors even though thus far they had only built experimental units of up to 5 megawatts. Those were euphoric days. The future of nuclear fission seemed assured and the Soviets were determined to explore each of its uses. The enthusiasm of the Soviet scientists was shared at the top political level. Premiers Nicolai Bulganin and Georgi Malenkov spoke of the 'century of atomic energy'. The Soviet peaceful programme now had its own momentum.

The Soviet Five Year Plan for 1956–60 included the world's most ambitious nuclear programme: between 2,000 and 2,500 megawatts of nuclear capacity by 1960. Only 400 megawatts would actually be finished. By contrast the British plan, drawn up in 1955, called first for 2,000 megawatts and then, a year later in the wake of the Suez fiasco, for 6,000 megawatts. The plan was revoked two years later. In America the twenty-year projection of nuclear generation capacity would be less than half fulfilled.

The exact turning point in the Soviet programme is not

known, but by 1959, the Minister for Power Stations was giving speeches that casually dismissed the prospects for nuclear power and emphasized the need to reduce costs. Kurchatov's successor, A. P. Alexandrov, admitted in 1962 that during the first plan 'practically all stations turned out to be more expensive than planned ... due mainly to the inexperience of the industry and changes in plans, but not due to technical reasons.' The changes in plans probably refers to the technological gamble of substantially increasing the size of the plants. The scientists were blamed for giving misleading cost projections.

The first major nuclear accident had also occurred at Kyshtym with the temporary loss of power of the Red Specialists. The Soviet public knew nothing of these concerns. Soviet literature is silent about standards of radiation protection in the early years of the bomb project, but the Soviet political leadership became acutely aware of the dangers of radioactivity in 1957. Malyshev died from leukaemia apparently some years after being exposed to radiation. Before he died, a German blood specialist was flown from Cologne to treat him.

Such evidence about safety standards as there is, admittedly self-serving to the west, suggests that the crash nuclear programme was one of the great public health disasters of the century. An early German refugee drew attention to the primitive protection standards in force at the Saxony uranium mines plundered by the Russians. US intelligence gathered many uncorroborated stories about deaths of sailors in the early Soviet nuclear submarines. Yet all the while the Soviets professed to make radiation protection their number one priority. In 1962, Alexandrov asserted that the 'main problem is the development of safe methods for utilizing nuclear energy. Its cost is the second most important problem.'

It was not until 1968, however, that Alexandrov emphasized the safety of contemporary reactors compared with the past and revealed that 'from 1946 through 1948, some of our employees got radiation cataracts of the eyes'. This was a stunning admission: cataracts were the earliest health effect to show up among those who survived the explosions at Hiroshima and Nagasaki. The effect does not generally occur unless the exposure has been as great as 200 rems or more. For industrial workers to have developed them suggests a huge, continuing health problem with a multiplication of leukaemias and cancers in the years ahead.

But worse was to come. In December 1957, or perhaps the first week of January 1958 – the exact date is not known – what was widely accepted in the west as the worst nuclear accident prior to Chernobyl occurred on the edge of the Siberian plain at the plutonium-producing complex at Kyshtym. The US Defense Intelligence Agency has identified Kyshtym as a reactor location that does not appear on the Soviet Union's published lists. In fact, the Russians have never admitted the accident occurred, but from scientific journals, intelligence reports and refugee accounts it has been possible to put together a reasonable picture of what happened. It is certain that lethal radioactivity spread over hundreds of miles and thousands had to be evacuated and resettled.

As in Chernobyl, but for different reasons, the first reports of the Kyshtym accident came from Scandinavia. Journalists in Denmark in April 1958, quoting diplomatic sources, wrote stories about a catastrophic accident inside the Soviet Union involving radioactive fall-out. The stories ran in the *New York Times*, but the US Atomic Energy Commission said it had 'no intelligence' of any such event. The next month, May, a newsletter published by the Munich-based Institute for the Study of the USSR, an arm of the propaganda unit of Radio Free Europe, commented on the 'unusual amount of attention' being given to radiation sickness in Soviet medical journals and even popular magazines. It said that on 9 January 1958, Radio Moscow had devoted a large segment to radiation sickness, describing in detail a list of possible preventive measures. This suggests that the accident happened around the end of December.

The accident was forgotten – or deliberately suppressed in the west – for nearly twenty years – until November 1976, when a Russian refugee biochemist, Zhores Medvedev, casually referred to the accident in the *New Scientist*. To his surprise he found that it was largely unknown. He suggested that the cause was probably an explosion, more likely chemical than nuclear, in radioactive wastes. His suggestion produced an hysterical reaction from western nuclear advocates because, at the time, the disposal of reactor wastes had become a major controversy in the western debate over nuclear power. It was an especially controversial issue in Britain. Medvedev was accused by intemperate British officials in the UK Atomic Energy Authority of being politically motivated in his explanation – especially as he had brought it up so long after the world had forgotten about it.

In fact, Medvedev, who was exiled from the Soviet Union in 1973 and lives in London, is a quiet, mild unassuming man. He is no militant Russian dissident. He had been asked by the *New Scientist* to write an article about Soviet science to commemorate the twentieth anniversary of Khrushchev's famous Party Congress speech denouncing Stalinism. Being a biochemist he had mentioned the Kyshtym disaster as an important historical dateline that brought the atomic physicists together with the long-persecuted geneticists. Medvedev's assertion that a large area of land had been contaminated was none the less soon confirmed. The CIA had documented some kind of nuclear accident in the southern Urals, but the most important evidence was found in the Soviet technical publications. Beginning in 1966, first a trickle then a stream of articles had appeared outlining in great detail ecological effects of radiation experiments. They were the result, it seemed, of a planned release of radio-activity. The radio-isotopes involved in the 'experiments', especially the large amount of strontium-90, pointed to nuclear wastes as the most likely source of the contamination. By 1979, American researchers, following Medvedev's lead, had identified no fewer than 115 articles in Soviet journals referring to these events. The most dramatic evidence came from a lake nicknamed 'Ilenko's Lake' for the Soviet scientist who had researched its underwater life after the accident. Studies of plankton, water plants and fish in this lake suggested a high contamination of radioactive strontium-90. An American reviewer described it as the most radioactive place on the face of the earth. In an unusual slip in Soviet censorship, one of Ilenko's studies, Medvedev found, said that the samples came from the Chelyabinsk region, which includes Kyshtym. Also, Medvedev discovered, nuclear wastes in storage could 'blow up' under special circumstances. One such process is described in a 1972 US Atomic Energy Commission report that investigated the accumulation of plutonium in wastes from the Hanford reactors in Washington State. Low-level radioactive wastes, which had been dumped in the unlined trenches in the hope that they would disperse harmlessly into the soil, had in fact produced a layer of highly concentrated plutonium. The layer was removed by the AEC, but the report suggested that a chain reaction could have been set off if water had soaked into the plutonium-rich soil. The rapid heating of the water could turn it into steam and the steam could have produced a 'mud-volcano type explosion'. Whatever the release mechanism, the accident appears to have involved the unintended release of reprocessed fission-product wastes. The number of people who died or who suffered radiation damage is not known. Reports by Soviet emigrants suggest that no public protection measures were taken until symptoms of acute radiation sickness were found – days after the accident. The government then ordered a hasty evacuation of the towns and villages where the effects were obvious. As hospitals throughout the region filled up, rest homes, clinics and hotels were hastily converted into health and evacuation centres. The major North–South highway through Kyshtym was closed for nine months. When it reopened, there were signs advising motorists not to stop for twenty miles and to drive at top speed with their windows closed.

A Soviet physicist who drove through the area two years after the accident later described the devastation.

> As far as I could see was empty land. The land was dead – no villages, no towns, only chimneys of destroyed homes, no cultivated fields or pastures, no herds, no people – nothing. It was like the moon for many hundreds of square kilometres, useless and unproductive for a very long time, maybe hundreds of years.

A decade later, local doctors were still advising pregnant women to have abortions. The region was still dotted with 'graveyards of the earth' – dumps for heavily irradiated topsoil – with clusters of 'giant mushrooms' growing behind the barbed wire. Food was still being checked for signs of radioactivity, and fishing in the lakes was still forbidden.

The second underlying cause for the disappearance of the initial Soviet nuclear programme was the declining political influence of the Red Specialists, the managerial elite of the atomic projects. They had reacted adversely to Khrushchev's campaign against Stalin and had moved against Khrushchev by creating a new 'economic cabinet' within the Politburo. Consisting of all the key technocrats, the new cabinet was intended to supervise economic decisions. Then, in June 1957, a majority of the Politburo, which included members of the economic cabinet, tried to dismiss Khrushchev, who, in an unprecedented move, appealed to the full central committee of the Party. With the logistical support of the military, Khrushchev flew a quorum of the committee to Moscow. The technocrats and their political supporters were denounced and dismissed as the 'anti-party group'.

Khrushchev's victory was the equivalent, in terms of communist ideology, of the reassertion of legislative control over the executive in a western parliamentary system. Denouncing the cadre of heavy industry specialists as 'steel eaters', Khrushchev proceeded to destroy their institutional power base. Twenty-five of the previously all-powerful central economic ministries in Moscow were abolished and their functions decentralized to regional economic councils. The key members of the managerial elite fell from grace, and thousands of economic administrators were dispatched to new jobs far from Moscow.

Although the atomic umbrella organization, the Ministry of Medium Machine Building, remained in existence, the political power of its administrators was smashed. The Five Year Plan, with its target of 2,500 megawatts by 1960 was abandoned. It was replaced in 1959 with a Seven Year Plan, which extended goals for most large engineering projects but ignored the targets for nuclear capacity. When Khrushchev outlined a new long-term plan for electricity up to 1980, nuclear generation was not mentioned at all. For as long as Khrushchev remained in command, no significant expansion of nuclear power was even discussed. The experimental units under construction were completed, but the Soviet rhetoric of an atomic age was restricted to presentations at international conferences.

The Russian nuclear scientists and engineers, with their

counterparts in America, Britain, Germany and France were going through what became known as the first 'ice age' of nuclear power. All the original grandiose targets of the mid-1950s turned out to be hopelessly optimistic. But that did not stop the nuclear zealots in these countries from continuing to produce atomic tricks. Americans dreamed of building an atomic airplane, and spent millions of dollars on it before acknowledging that it would never fly because the lead shield for the on-board reactor made the craft too heavy to take off. The Russians themselves led the way into nuclear marine craft with merchant ship nuclear propulsion. They launched their icebreaker, *Lenin*, in the summer of 1960. Politically the Soviet nuclear establishment had suffered a severe setback, but for technological optimists in Russia the vision of a nuclear future was still as bright as it ever was.

The revival came after Khrushchev's overthrow in October 1964. The old Red Specialists Khrushchev had suppressed began reappearing at the centre of the Soviet elite. Within a year the official campaign for nuclear power was in full swing again, with a series of government promotion articles, new cost estimates and a highly publicized launch of a biography of Kurchatov. The Red Specialists, like their counterparts in the west, claimed they had improved the efficiency of nuclear power. It would now be cost effective compared with other forms of energy.

By 1968, the Soviet utility planners were sufficiently convinced of the economics to begin a modest expansion of nuclear power, and the special atomic power division of the Ministry of Power was revived. After looking at various reactor types the Soviets concentrated on two basic technologies. One was based on the early, small reactors of the light-water cooled, graphite moderated 'channel' type that became known as the RBMK. The Soviets gave up production of these temporarily when they were proving costly and difficult and switched to the second design, the pressurized water-cooled type, or PWR. These were similar to the successful design made by Westinghouse in America. The Soviet PWR is known as the WWER, or 'water, water, energetics reactor'. But in 1970 a group of American scientists visiting the Soviet Union were surprised to learn that the Soviets had revived the old RBMK design, and next they were touting the reactor's safety record. In 1983, Boris Semenov, the Soviet head of the Department of Nuclear Safety at the International Atomic Energy Agency (IAEA) singled out the new design features of the RBMK for special praise. 'Having more than 1,000 individual primary circuits increases the safety of the reactor system [and] a serious loss of coolant accident is practically impossible,' he wrote in a paper entitled, 'Nuclear Power in the Soviet Union'.

According to Soviet scientists the RBMK reactors reduce problems associated with breakdown in the individual 'channels' or tubes making up the core of the reactor, because a channel can be replaced without shutting down the entire reactor. But there was another reason why this type of reactor was of special use to the Soviets. Semenov hinted at the reason in the same 1983 paper. 'Because of the good physical characteristics of the reactor and the on-load refuelling system,' he wrote, 'low-enriched fuel can be used with high efficiency. The discharged fuel has a low fissionable material content. The burn-up is high, and the plutonium produced in the fuel is utilized.' To a nuclear engineer this means that the reactor can be used for producing weapons-grade plutonium. 'On-load' refuelling means that the reactor can be refuelled without shutting it down, and frequent replacement of the fuel rods is necessary to minimize the build-up of isotopes undesirable for weapons-grade plutonium. Because the RBMK can be used in this way the Soviets do not export them. All their exports are PWRs. At the beginning of 1983, 27 Soviet PWRs were in operation throughout Russia and the Eastern Bloc countries, including 13 units in Bulgaria, Czechoslovakia, the German Democratic Republic and Hungary. There are 28 RBMKs operating inside the Soviet Union.

In 1971 the 24th CPSU congress inserted a new nuclear target into the ninth Five Year Plan. It called for an expansion of the existing capacity of 1,600 megawatts by adding 6–8,000 megawatts in five years. The congress resolution even specified that the extra capacity should be in the new 1,000 megawatt units. Although the ninth Five Year Plan did not meet its target, the planners continued to be as ambitious in the tenth, covering the 1976–80 period. At this time the west was going through its second nuclear 'ice age' – mainly because of an economic recession, but also because of opposition to nuclear power from environmental movements.

By contrast, the Soviet programme was spurred on by another dynamic. Exports of oil and natural gas account for nearly 80 per cent of the Soviet Union's hard currency income. At the end of the 1970s, the Soviet leadership began to be concerned that production of oil and natural gas might not be sufficient to meet both domestic and foreign targets. In 1979 Premier Kosygin called for the eventual complete displacement of petroleum products as fuel for low-potential heat and electricity. This was, in effect, a command for nuclear power to take a greater share of electricity production. The Soviets surged ahead, hoping to bring into operation between 13 and 15,000 megawatts by 1980, and they announced plans to construct facilities to enable them to build 10,000 megawatts each year during the 1980s.

In addition to the PWRs and the RBMKs, the Soviets also tested their first prototype commercial breeder reactor, the BN 350, in 1972. Fuelled by plutonium, the breeder produces more plutonium than it consumes. By 1980, a larger BN 600 had been commissioned at Beloyarske, and they are working on a gigantic BN 1600-megawatt breeder. In addition, according to the CIA, the Soviets already have a 'stretched' Chernobyl-type RBMK with a capacity of 1,500 megawatts. It started up in late 1983 at Ignalina, Lithuania. The eleventh and twelfth Five Year Plans up to 1990 continued the upward trend of nuclear power. Compared with the west's sharp downturn, the Soviet record is impressive: by 1982 the total installed capacity of nuclear power plants exceeded 18,000 megawatts. In total, the Soviet Union now has a nuclear generating capacity of 28,000 megawatts, which accounted for 11 per cent of the nation's total power output, placing the Soviets third in countries with nuclear power, behind the United States and France. This is indeed a considerable achievement in a country where construction delays are legendary and often provide material for western mockery about the short-comings of a communist command economy. But beneath the impressive array of figures lies a heap of trouble, including a series of relatively minor accidents and the first important internal voices of dissent about the way the nuclear power programme was being planned.

To cope with the enormous demand for nuclear reactor parts and also for nuclear fuel materials, the Soviets embarked on an extraordinary, and, in the end, disastrous, technological adventure – an enormous complex of factories, known as Atommash, or atomic power machinery complex, at Volgodonsk, outside Moscow. The 'all nuclear' complex, a sort of supermarket of nuclear reactor parts, used electricity generated by its own nuclear reactors and was staffed on a round-the-clock schedule by 28,000 workers. The Soviets hoped that the complex, under the newly created Ministry of Power Machinery, would reduce delays and postponements caused by inter-ministry foul-ups. But the complex had only been opened for two years when, in 1983, the Soviets discovered it was built too close to a water reservoir, causing the plant's foundation to be undermined. Medvedev comments, 'The disaster was huge, never before experienced in Soviet industry. A commission was set up by Yuri Andropov to investigate the situation. The secretary of the Central Committee and a candidate member of the Politburo, Vladimir Dolgikh, flew to Volgodonsk to lead the study. The findings of the commission were never made public, but the chairman of the State Construction Committee was immediately dismissed and many other officials followed him, some into retirement, some into prison. It was found that many parts for the atomic industry were of poor quality, pipes were substandard, metal was not according to specifications.' According to Medvedev, the Politburo discussed the affair in more detail and recommended a new state committee, the Committee on the Supervision of the Safety of the Works in the Atomic Energy System. It is the only state committee besides the KGB that does not have its own professional journal. Says Medvedev, 'Its findings and recommendations are too hot to be discussed openly.'

But bad news has leaked out. A few months before Atommash opened, *Nucleonics Week*, a US nuclear industry newsletter, noted reports in the newspaper, *Socialist Industry*, complaining that large quantities of precast panelling had been delivered to the Chernobyl site in the wrong sizes and that the plant had been unable to secure delivery of eight tonnes of ordinary bolts because the supplier was short of steel. These problems, and others of poor management and supply bottlenecks apparently affected the building of unit three at Chernobyl. (The accident happened in unit four.)

Apart from these delays, the list of relatively minor accidents has been growing at Soviet nuclear plants since 1979. That year the Soviet Minister of Energy and Electrification told visiting US congressmen of two incidents. In one, a cooling line fractured, spilling radioactive water on to the floor of a reactor containment vessel. In another, a steam generator ruptured and radioactive steam spread into the facility. The identity of the reactors is not known. In 1982, unofficial Soviet sources confirmed that an unspecified accident had occurred at one of the units of the Rovno PWR reactors. In 1983 the Soviets reported a fire in the Armenskaya plant in Soviet Armenia. The fire was in electrical cables but had serious consequences, apparently, because the reactor control and power cables were located in the same cable lines.

Some of these warning signals – the 'sound of the tocsin', as Gorbachev would characterize the Chernobyl accident – seemed to have dented the brash optimism of the Soviet nuclear establishment. Early Soviet nuclear reactors were not enclosed in containment vessels, the large-dome-shaped structures designed to prevent release of radioactivity in the event of an accident at the nuclear core. But, in 1980, the first such vessel was built for a PWR at the Novo-Voronezhsky plant.

In other aspects of nuclear safety, according to western observers, the Soviets have been extraordinarily cavalier. Solid wastes are said to have been dumped into the Black Sea, for example. Another practice which has drawn criticism from within the Soviet Union itself is the siting of reactors close to urban centres. Part of the reason for this is the twin purpose of several Soviet reactors, of heating water to make steam to turn turbines and also to supply communities with steam heat. Since steam does not travel long distances, such reactors must be built in the centre of the communities they serve. One such plant is at Gorky. In a September 1979 article on power plant construction that appeared in the high-level party theoretical journal, *Kommunist*, two respected Soviet scientists, N. Dollozhal and Y. Koryakin discuss, apparently as spokesmen for what would seem to be a substantial body within the party, the wisdom of siting nuclear power plants near the centres of population and farmland. The fact that they wrote in *Kommunist* was evidence that an argument was raging within the establishment between responsible scientists and the late President Brezhnev's economic planners. The argument was settled, in the time-honoured way, 18 months later by another article in the same journal by Anatoly Alexandrov, the 83-year-old President of the Academy of Sciences. He declared that properly supervised power plants were 100 per cent safe, and should be sited as close as possible to urban centres to provide winter heating.

When he was in Moscow in 1979, the Governor of Pennsylvania, Dick Thornborough, made, it seems, an astute analogy between the older members of the Soviet nuclear establishment, like Alexandrov, and the early zealots of nuclear power in the west who were more interested in promoting nuclear power than regulating it. He was right to wonder whether the March 1979 accident at Three Mile Island would make a difference in the Soviet Union. Would the unbridled enthusiasm for and unwavering devotion to nuclear power of the old Red Specialists be moved by questions of safety raised by a serious accident – particularly if it happened on their own doorstep?

5 The accident

'The plants are safe: it's the people who aren't.'
John Kemeny, chairman of US commission that
investigated the nuclear accident at Three Mile Island,
31 October 1979

Near the meeting of the rivers Uzh and Pripyat, there stands
an uninspiring, simple one-storey building. This is Chernobyl weather station, one of a chain that crosses the
Ukraine and which provides forecasts for Russian farmers.
There, Soviet scientists work in the secluded calm of a
remote, relatively unimportant meteorology centre. Eight
times a day, the six station workers carry out a ritual of
checking wind flow and direction, of analysing soil moisture
and of observing cloud movements – standard procedures
that are familiar routine for meteorologists throughout the
world.

But in the early hours of Saturday 26 April, that calm
routine was abruptly disrupted. At the time, station chief
Zinaida Kordyk was carrying out morning measurements.
Carefully, she took down the different readings, as she had
done on countless previous occasions, until she stopped at
one piece of equipment – the station's Geiger counter. To
her horror, the counter was giving a reading that showed
there was a sudden and severe increase in radiation levels
outside her station.

An experienced meteorologist, Kordyk knew that rapid
rise could only mean one thing. 'There was only one explanation – something had gone badly wrong at the
Chernobyl atom plant,' she recalls.

Kordyk's assessment was to prove to be horribly accurate. Her discovery also has historical significance. She was the first person outside the stricken atom plant to discover that its deadly outpourings had already begun their journey across Europe. The readings on the weather station's dials were, however, a pale shadow of the dark cloud that was about to cover Europe.

Indeed by late Saturday morning, much of reactor No. 4 and its surrounding buildings were fiercely ablaze. Vast plumes of highly radioactive debris were being hurled high into the atmosphere.

No accident has ever rivalled its severity. But what on earth triggered such a calamity?

Many western newspapers later speculated wildly about explanations and causes. Few of their theories have subsequently survived close scrutiny. Indeed, Soviet authorities took weeks merely to establish the basic sequence of events that occurred that morning.

Details of that sequence were first given by Soviet leader, Mikhail Gorbachev, on 14 May. 'During planned decommissioning of the No. 4 generating set, the power of the reactor suddenly increased,' he stated. 'The considerable discharge of steam and subsequent reaction led to the formation of hydrogen, its explosion, the destruction of the reactor and the radioactive emission connected with it.'

Such a stark description gave little away. Gorbachev was probably still unaware of the appalling catalogue of operators' errors at the plant. In fact, there had been 'deliberate, systematic and numerous violations of procedure', a long and frank Soviet report informed the International Atomic Energy Authority conference on the accident. This was backed by an even franker speech by the leader of the Soviet delegation, Academician Valery Legasov; and the combined picture they painted was one of devastating complacency and irresponsibility.

At the time, the reactor was due to be shut down for annual maintenance. Its operators decided to use the opportunity to test how long the power station's steam turbines could generate electricity after its steam supply had been shut off. Legasov revealed that there 'had been a lot of discussion concerning the justification of the test.' Nevertheless, they had decided to go ahead. The operators wanted to be sure that — in the event of an accidental cut-off of the steam — the turbines could continue to generate power which was needed to keep the reactor's safety systems working. The power station did have emergency diesel generators, but these took time to start up, and in the interval the free-wheeling turbines would have to carry the load. Two previous experiments at Chernobyl reactors, in 1982 and 1984, had shown the turbines could not supply the necessary electricity before the diesel generators cut in. So new equipment, designed to solve the problem, was installed and a test was arranged.

But the technicians who drew up the plans did not discuss them with the physicists or other nuclear safety staff at the plant, though they did send experiment plans to the designers of the power station. However, the designers did not get round to looking at them, and never issued any authorisation for the experiment. Yet the tests proceeded.

And from the beginning, the operators seemed hell-bent on self-destruction. Their first serious error was to switch off the emergency core cooling system. This was unnecessary and meant that the reactor would be without one of its most vital safety systems. It was the first of six 'dangerous violations' of the Chernobyl operating rules. It did not cause the accident, but it made its consequences more severe.

The official report also revealed that 'the operators involved were not adequately prepared for the tests, and were not aware of the possible dangers.' This failure was to have grim consequences. When things began to go wrong, operators overrode one fail-safe system after another — any one of which could have prevented the accident occurring.

At 1 a.m. on Friday, 25 April — almost exactly 24 hours before the accident was to occur — operators began the task of gradually reducing the power of reactor No. 4. They were aiming to bring it down from 3,200 MW (thermal) to between 700 and 1,000 MW, the level set for the experiment. By lunchtime, it had reached 1,600 MW, and at 2 p.m. they switched off the emergency cooling system.

But then the operators received an urgent call from the local grid controller at Kiev. He needed the reactor's electricity for several more hours, and told the operators to stop running down the power. They obeyed, but failed to turn the emergency cooling back on again. So the reactor went on running without this crucial safety system — a clear violation of the rules.

At 11.10 p.m. the grid controller said he no longer needed the electricity, and the operators returned to reducing the reactor's power. Then at 28 minutes past midnight, on April 26, the operators made another simple, fateful error. They forgot to set a regulator properly. 'This is the kind of operator error that we all experience in our plants, and it is difficult to eliminate,' said Dr Pierre Tanguy, chairman of the commission that examined the accident sequence at the conference. 'But without it, there would have been no accident.' It was the second crucial violation of safety procedures.

As a result of the incorrect regulator setting, the reactor's power slumped dramatically. Instead of stabilising at 700—1,000 MW, it crashed to 30 MW — far too low for the test. At this point the operators should have simply abandoned the experiment and closed the reactor down. But they decided to try to rescue it. Their motive was straightforward. If the experiment had been abandoned, it could not have been repeated for another year when the reactor would have been next shut down for maintenance. The senior authorities who had ordered the test would have been furious and would have found out the regulator error. So the operators decided, literally, to pull out the stops to try to restore the reactor's power.

But they faced a major problem — a phenomenon called 'xenon poisoning'. Xenon-135, a gas, is one of the fission products produced during reactor operation. It absorbs neutrons, the lifeblood of nuclear fission. During full-power operation, there are enough neutrons to overcome this absorption. But at very low power, xenon build-up is a dominating factor.

This led to the operators' third dangerous violation. They started pulling out control rods. The plant's operating rules state there should never be less than 30 control rods at one time, though a minimum of 15 is occasionally permitted. In their desperation, however, the operators removed rods until there were only six to eight left in the core.

By 1 a.m. the power had climbed to 200 MW, which was still far too low for the experiment. Yet the operators decided to press ahead with the test — and made their fourth violation. At 1.03 and 1.07 they switched on two extra pumps to join the six that were already circulating cooling water through the core. This was a measure laid down in the test programme. Under normal conditions, it would have added to the safety of the reactor, but at this low power it crucially altered the balance of steam and water in the circuit and made the reactor, in Legasov's words, 'extremely unstable'.

Water and steam levels began changing unpredictably from second to second, and the operators could not control them. And then they made their fifth major mistake. At about 1.20 a.m., in response to steam pressures that were sagging and to the water level that was dropping below the emergency mark, they blocked the automatic shut-down system that would normally have closed down the reactor.

At 1.23 a.m. they started the experiment. Four seconds later they performed the sixth, and final, violation. They switched off the last safety system which would have come into operation automatically when the turbines shut down. Their motives are unclear, but whatever they were, the operators had now closed the last mechanism that might have prevented disaster.

The reactor was now running free, isolated from the outside world, its control rods out, and its safety systems disconnected. As Legasov told the Vienna conference: 'The reactor was free to do as it wished'.

It took the shift manager just 30 seconds to realise something was seriously wrong. He shouted at an operator to press button AZ—5. This should have driven all the control and scram rods into the core. The rods fell, but did not go fully home, probably because the fuel or the rods were already distorted by heat. 'Banging noises' were heard, and the rods were disconnected to allow them to fall into the core by their own weight. But it was too late.

In the last second of the reactor's life its power surged from 7 per cent to several hundred times its normal level. A small part of the reactor's core went 'prompt critical'. The effect was the equivalent of half a ton of TNT exploding in the core. In fact, it was very like the detonation of an atomic bomb — something that the nuclear industry had always insisted could never happen in a reactor. (The main difference is that in a bomb the reaction goes much faster, taking only a few billionths of a second.) Disaster struck so fast that the fuel did not have time to melt — it simply shattered into fragments.

Four seconds later a second explosion occurred. The Vienna conference could not agree on its cause, however. Some experts thought it must have been a repetition of the first one. The Soviet scientists disagreed, insisting it was caused by steam. Whatever the causes, the explosions blasted the 1,000-tonne lid clean off the reactor, and brought the giant 200-tonne refuelling crane crashing down on the core, destroying more cooling circuits. Within seconds, the zirconium cladding of the fuel rods began to react with the steam to form hydrogen. This was to cause, as the official Russian report describes it, 'a fireworks display of glowing particles and fragments escaping from the units'. It set off 30 separate fires in the building. The huge blocks of graphite in the reactor core also caught fire.

The entire deadly sequence was summed up with admirable brevity in the Russian report, which said: 'The continuing reduction of water flow through the fuel channels as the power rose led to intensive steam formation and then to nucleate boiling, over-heating of the fuel, destruction of the fuel, a rapid surge of coolant boiling with particles of destroyed fuel entering the coolant, a rapid and abrupt increase of pressure in the fuel channels, destruction of the fuel channels, and finally an explosion which destroyed the reactor and part of the building and released radioactive fission products into the environment.'

This explanation is now the accepted expert account of the disaster. But for many months, engineers in the west could only guess about the causes of the world's worst nuclear accident. At the time many other theories were suggested. Some scientists said mistakes in fuel rod positions triggered the power surge. Uranium fuel at various levels of enrichment is used inside reactors. This is done to prevent fission heat being concentrated in the very heart of a core. Instead, more reactive, enriched fuel is used near the reactor's rim to spread the heat flux. However, if several rods of enriched fuel had been placed together in the Chernobyl reactor, local criticality might have built up there. In addition, some French and American scientists thought that a turbine failure, which sent fragments spinning into the reactor core, might have set off the accident, while others proposed that a pressure tube failure, which would have blocked coolant flow, led to local over-heating. Other American sources suggested that a fire in the turbine room could have been the triggering event. However, the theory had to rely on a simultaneous loss of coolant occurring in the reactor, for no apparent reason. The theory also assumed, wrongly, that the RBMK had no active cooling system which would have been able to counter the effects of the loss of coolant. The inability of experts to pinpoint the cause of the Chernobyl disaster was understandable. No-one could have expected that the true cause would turn out to be such a wild catalogue of wilful human error.

By now the entire Chernobyl complex was facing complete destruction. 'Fire had broken out in over 30 places as a result of the explosions in the reactor, which had ejected fragments of its core, heated to high temperatures, onto the roofs above several areas housing the reactor section, the de-aeration stages and the machine hall. Because of damage to some oil pipes, electric cable short circuits and the intense heat radiation from the reactor, focuses of fire formed in the machine hall over turbogenerator number 7, in the reactor hall and in the adjoining, partially destroyed buildings,' the official report stated.

The fate of Chernobyl reactor No. 4 was now sealed. Its double containment was breached and the top of its core had been smashed open. Broken pressure tubes were no longer providing coolant to the top of the core, which continued to overheat, triggering further reactions between the steam that now poured over the reactor's zirconium and its red-hot blocks of graphite. The graphite itself caught fire and began pouring out plumes of highly radioactive fission products — such as lanthanum-140, ruthenium-103, caesium-137, iodine-131, tellurium-132, strontium-89, strontium-90, and yttrium-91 — which Soviet scientists later found contaminating the surrounding countryside. The cloud escaped through a gaping hole in the reactor hall roof and into the night. In addition, fire began to spread to reactor No. 3 and threatened to spark an even greater calamity. Only human bravery and self-sacrifice prevented that from happening.

A minute after the fatal surge had begun to wreak its dreadful damage, the first warnings were sounded. The duty crew of the No. 2 military fire-fighting unit heard a roar. A second later their quarters echoed to the howl of sirens. The crew struggled into their protective gear and raced towards their vehicles. By the time they reached the plant, the blaze had already taken a grip. 'In the reactor hall, flames were raging on various floors, at five points at least, including the roof and the adjoining turbine hall,' recalled Leonid Telyatnikov, the Chernobyl fire chief, from his hospital bed in Moscow.

As soon as Telyatnikov had arrived at the burning reactor building, racing from his home 6 km away, he saw that the 28 firefighters already there were losing against the fire. The flames were threatening to spread through the cable channels to other parts of the reactor complex, including nearby reactor No. 3.

Telyatnikov split his men into groups and several times led one group by climbing to the highest part of the station roof where the turbine section towers 69 metres above the ground. This section was the most seriously ablaze.

Here the Soviet firemen showed the extraordinary heroism that was to become the hallmark of their battle to contain the Chernobyl reactor fire. All knew radiation must be leaking from the damaged reactor core for dosimetric emergency teams had already warned of the danger. None flinched from his task. 'The fire had to be fought whatever happened,' said Telyatnikov. At this point, he and his men were struggling to combat a blaze in desperate conditions. Fumes and smoke were pouring from the blazing hall below while the bitumen on the turbine hall roof melted rapidly in the intense heat. Soon the men found their boots were becoming heavier by the minute. Their feet were caught in the molten mass and turned 'leaden' as the resin stuck.

Under these conditions, the firemen fought the blaze for three hours, until they halted the spread of the flames and prevented fire damaging Chernobyl's three other operational reactors. The actions of these men undoubtedly saved a far greater disaster from occurring, as the other technicians struggled to shut down the whole power station, and put the three adjoining reactors on emergency stand-by cooling. They could not be abandoned, however fierce were the waves of radioactivity and fire that surrounded them. Those on duty that night would later pay dearly for their heroism.

Telyatnikov had already summoned support from Kiev Region fire headquarters, which ordered all units to the reactor. Among the fire leaders who first arrived was Lieutenant Ivan Saureye. It was immediately clear to Saureye that many of the firemen on the roof were by this time in a very bad state, having fought the fire in smoke and intense radiation for several hours. Saureye and his men brought the fire team down to the ground on ladders and had them taken away in ambulances before taking their places on the roof. For twenty minutes they continued to spray the roof of No. 3 reactor hall with water to prevent it from igniting from the heat of the blaze in No. 4, before being forced to come down themselves.

Saureye and Telyatnikov were later taken to the same hospital ward. A Soviet journalist interviewing the two men was told by the hospital staff: 'We do not abandon hope that they will recover,' although by that time six of their colleagues were already dead from the effects of the radiation that poured over them that night.

The first victim of Chernobyl was Valeriy Hodiemchuk. Described simply as a power station operator, Hodiemchuk was pinned beneath collapsing masonry at his work station as the explosion went off. Nearby his fellow worker and friend, Vladimir Sashionok, who was described as the auto-system setter, was also caught in the blast. Staggering from the wrecked block with 80 per cent burns, Sashionok fell into the arms of horrified workmates and gasped only two words, 'Valeriy. Inside', before losing consciousness. Sashionok died in the ambulance. He never had a funeral. The ambulance crew, fearing radioactive contamination, buried him on the spot, in the cemetery of the first village that they came to.

Such small tragedies put the devastating events at Chernobyl in a particularly chilling perspective. But how could the accident have been allowed to happen in the first place? Scientists now know what caused it. Why could they not have foreseen disaster?

The answer is, as Legasov put it in Vienna, that the extraordinary series of deliberate operator violations was, quite simply, 'impossible to foresee'. He described their behaviour as the 'pilot of a plane deciding to test it while flying very high, by opening the doors and switching off the safety systems'. And he added with some justice: 'I do not think any designer of the plane could foresee that'.

Human error — or, rather, astonishing human recklessness — was therefore the overwhelming cause of the Chernobyl disaster. However, Legasov did also admit to some 'shortcomings' in the design of the reactor. The most important of these was the problem of the 'positive void coefficient' in the reactor core. This made it easier for part of the core to run out of control, as it did at Chernobyl, and make possible the near-nuclear explosion. In a positive void, the hotter the reactor becomes, the more steam is generated in the core; and the more steam that is generated, the faster the nuclear reaction proceeds — and so the reactor gets even hotter. PWRs also use water as a coolant but are so designed that the reactor will slow down the hotter the water gets.

This shortcoming was recognised in the early days of the reactor's design. Safety systems were incorporated to protect against it — the ones that were over-ridden by the operators on the night of April 25.

Legasov also admitted that the Soviet Union should have placed more reliance on automatic control systems and less on human initiative, in designing the RBMK. And he gave an intriguing reason for this mistake. When the reactor type was first developed, automatic systems were thought to be too unreliable. 'This accident shows a tremendous psychological mistake on the behalf of the designers, that they did not foresee the protective system that might be capable of preventing an accident in the case of a number of switching-offs of the means of control in violation of the operational rules,' Legasov said.

Western nuclear chiefs have been quick to exploit these admissions. Lord Marshall, head of the nationalised English electricity utility, the CEGB, claimed that Legasov was 'admitting faults in design, in training, in Soviet safety philosophy'. And at the end of the conference he declared that Britain had nothing to learn about the design or about the operation of nuclear plants as a result of the Chernobyl accident — a reaction entirely consistent with the West's general reaction to the accident.

Indeed, in the immediate aftermath of the accident, nuclear authorities across the world acted with almost indecent haste to distance themselves from the Chernobyl accident. 'It couldn't happen here. We design much better plants and we take greater care about safety,' was the continual response of utility and reactor programme chiefs speaking on television and radio and to newspaper reporters. For instance, within hours of the full story of the disaster breaking in Britain, Marshall was calmly reassuring TV viewers that such an accident was highly improbable in Britain. A few days later, he was reassuring the annual lunch of the British Nuclear Forum with the same message.

There is nothing like the Chernobyl reactor anywhere in the civil nuclear power in the western world. The reactor it *least resembles* is the PWR proposed for Sizewell. A reactor superficially similar to Chernobyl, but with great advantages over it, failed to get past British safety criteria in the 1970s.

Amid the brandy, cigars and coffee, his comforting words were received like a prophet's promise of salvation to the faithful. The anxious agency chiefs and civil engineers who make up the personnel of the nuclear industry have a great deal to lose if there were a major collapse of faith in their product.

In their defence, western nuclear barons do have some strong facts. One of their most powerful pieces of evidence was quickly produced by the British electricity board — in the form of an investigation of safety and operating standards of the RBMK. The investigation was made by a delegation of scientists from the UK Nuclear Power Company, the forerunner of the present National Nuclear Corporation. They visited Russia in October and November 1975 and concentrated their attention on the RBMK that was already operating in Leningrad. It was not an easy task, however. The team found that the Russian data that they were given was 'not always comprehensive or easily understood'. The group therefore faced serious problems in analysis and assessment. Nevertheless, they did come to a fairly gloomy conclusion — that the RBMK was not a satisfactory plant by British standards.

Their report stated:
The Leningrad reactors do not have the containment vessel, channel spray system and secondary shutdown

system as used in the UK. . . . However, the most important problem seems to be that of designing and demonstrating a core restraint system that could resist the steam pressure in the event of a pressure tube rupturing.

These flaws still apply to RBMKs, including those at Chernobyl, although it was not immediately realized in the west that the Chernobyl design incorporates many safety refinements which improved substantially on the old Leningrad design. International nuclear inspectors do not feel the RBMK's characteristics necessarily imply dangerous design problems. Certainly, they do not view them as the inherently unsafe, unlicensable heaps of junk that some western nuclear engineers have subsequently claimed them to be. 'Intuitively, I feel they are a little more difficult and have a few more design problems than some western reactors — but the difference is not very great,' said one leading inspector. 'The PWR is also difficult to operate.'

Nevertheless, some important questions still have to be answered about the standard of operation of the RBMK. The most important of these centres on the temperature of its core while it is running. This is given by the Russians as being 550 °C, with peaks or 'hot spots' reaching 750 °C. 'This is an astonishingly high temperature,' said Dr Eric Voice, a nuclear expert based at Dounreay, in Scotland. 'At temperatures like that, you will find all sorts of unwelcome effects beginning to occur inside the reactor.' For one thing, zirconium approaches a temperature at which it loses structural strength. Indeed, at 700 °C, it would be well on its way to reaching a temperature at which it would start to react with steam to produce hydrogen. And in the presence of air, graphite gets close to its burning point. Running the reactor between 550 and 700 °C (compared with much cooler graphite cores used in British reactors) severely reduces safety margins in the RBMK. In addition, the use of water and graphite in the same reactor has also been criticized as being an unstable combination.

On the other hand, the RBMK has substantial safety advantages over western reactors. Its honeycomb of individual primary coolant circuits is a major advantage because they make the prospect of a serious loss of coolant accident extremely unlikely. In addition, the separation of the fuel into a myriad different channels is also a benefit as this makes a full meltdown (which did not happen at Chernobyl) unlikely The fuel will not fall to the bottom in one radioactive mass but will separate into small portions (which in fact did happen at Chernobyl). This compares with the PWR which has its fuel all 'in one pot' and is therefore more vulnerable to a complete meltdown. In addition, a confidential Nuclear Regulatory Commission report on the Chernobyl accident makes it clear that reactor No. 4 had substantial containment facilities. The first concrete containment box surrounded the reactor and portions of the inlet and outlet water piping. Its design pressure was 27 psi (pounds per square inch). The second containment region enclosed the major diameter piping and headers of the system. The largest pipe in this volume was 90 cm (35 inch) in diameter. This region had a design pressure of 57 psi.

The point remains that all nuclear reactors have different strengths and weaknesses, and designers have to maximise the former and minimise the latter. But it is hard to see how any designer can protect a reactor against overweening human folly. As Legasov pointed out, if the operators had only foreborne from any one of the last five of their six violations, the accident would not have taken place.

And in the end, the most remarkable lesson to emerge from the accident is a psychological one. The Chernobyl No. 4 reactor was one of the best in the country, and its operators had a good reputation for reliability. And that, the Vienna conference concluded, was the main reason for the accident.

Dr Brian Edmondson said in his official summing up that the operators had 'lost their fear of the reactor' and 'lost all sense of danger'. This was probably because their previous record had led to 'dominant overconfidence.'

As the chairman of the State Committee of the USSR for the Utilisation of Nuclear Energy, A. M. Petrosyants, reported: 'It may well be that the uninterrupted working of the power station led to a certain complacency and placidity and this might to a certain extent indirectly have been the cause of the irresponsibility, negligence and lack of discipline that did — in the final count — lead to such serious consequences.'

'Those responsible for the accident have been meted out a serious punishment, but the lesson taught us by Chernobyl will remind us for a long time to come how vital it is to have a strict, careful, precautionary attitude to technology in general and to new technology in particular.'

The bizarre and sudden tombs of Valeriy Hodiemchuk and Vladimir Sashionok are as telling monuments as any to that fatal fallibility of nuclear technology. For more than a week, the two men's deaths were the only ones to which the Soviet authorities would admit — and that of Hodiemchuk prompted one of the few poignant stories to be published about the disaster in the Soviet press. Before going on night duty, Hodiemchuk told his wife the family would travel that weekend to the next village, there to help his mother plant potatoes. When the weekend came, Hodiemchuk's wife and small son did travel on a bus to the village just as planned. His little boy still thought his father was on duty at the plant. And so he was. But the bus was in an evacuation convoy, fleeing the radiation of Chernobyl. And Hodiemchuk would never be able to leave his duty at the plant. His body was to be covered in cement and abandoned inside. The huge concrete sarcophagus being built over the No. 4 reactor will make an awesome tombstone for his son to visit: as it will too, for his own children and his children's children in turn — on through the many centuries it will take for Hodiemchuk's grave to become safe.

6 How the world found out

'We are in a capitalist country now.'
US Congressman Edward J. Markey, to Vitaly Churkin,
second secretary at the Soviet embassy, during the Capitol
Hill hearing on Chernobyl, 1 May 1986

An enduring irony of the Chernobyl accident is that it was first detected by Sweden, a country committed to dismantling its 12 nuclear power plants by the year 2010. At 2 p.m. on Sunday afternoon, 27 April, a radioactive cloud, riding on south-westerly winds at about 5,000 feet drifted silently and unannounced across Sweden's southernmost shores. The Geiger counters at the unmanned radiation monitors scattered around Sweden's borders began registering an increase in radioactivity – but not enough to cause an alarm. For a politically neutral country, Sweden is surprisingly equipped with an extraordinary array of snooping devices. Off the coast float the latest acoustic gadgets to ferret out Soviet submarines often believed, and sometimes found, lurking in the deep Swedish fjords. Inland, the seismic laboratory at Uppsala tracks Soviet underground nuclear explosions, while above ground sampling sensors are constantly sniffing for radioactive fall-out. In the air, Swedish air force jet fighters make regular radioactivity sampling flights at various altitudes. The network of sensors was set up in 1963, primarily to monitor the international compliance with the treaty banning atmospheric nuclear tests.

At 9 a.m. on Monday, 28 April a worker arrived at the Forsmark nuclear power plant, north of Stockholm on the east coast of Sweden, and routinely stuck his feet into the installation's radiation detector. It set off an alarm that sounded around the world – the dust on the blue covers on the worker's shoes was radioactive. Bengt Hellman, the plant's safety inspector, at first thought that the worker had come from a restricted zone and had been careless with safety regulations. But the man had not been into any radioactive areas: he had brought the dust into the plant from the outside.

The plant was immediately evacuated and, suspecting a fault in their own reactors, the plant's engineers searched frantically for a leak. A radio warning was broadcast to local residents telling them to keep away from Forsmark and police road blocks were set up to turn back motorists. When the sensors failed to detect anything unusual, they lined up the plant's 700 workers and tested them with a Geiger counter – the workers' clothing set the counter clicking to between five and ten times normal background radiation levels.

To the north and east, rain and a gentle spring snow were falling over parts of Finland and Sweden where similar readings of increased radioactivity were being recorded. The prevailing wind patterns showed that the source of the radiation had to be the Soviet Union. For several days currents of air had been flowing from the Black Sea and into Scandinavia.

The Swedes contacted the Americans, who suggested that the radioactivity could have come from a Soviet underground test that had somehow vented. Over the last 23 years, using information from the Swedish sensors and its own air patrol monitoring, the United States has detected traces of radioactivity in clouds outside the Soviet Union on almost 200 occasions. According to the Pentagon, in about 100 of these there were indications that radioactive gases and small particles had escaped from Soviet underground tests. (Ninety-seven underground weapons tests in the United States also resulted in release of radioactive gases during between 1964 and 70.) The American suggestion was a cynical one. The Soviets are in the middle of a much-publicized self-imposed nuclear test moratorium, which the United States has declined to join because testing is an integral part of its nuclear weapons build-up. Washington's first answer to the riddle of the cloud was, in part, genuine bafflement and, in part, wishful thinking by administration hardliners who would like to see the Kremlin end the moratorium – and thus put a stop to the criticism directed at the United States for continuing to test.

In fact, the Swedes had already determined that it was not a Soviet test. For one thing there had been no movement on their seismic monitors, for another the radioactivity sensors were picking up material not associated with weapons tests. 'It was immediately apparent that the radioactivity was not due to a nuclear weapons test because of the particular combination of certain isotopes, such as cobalt, iodine and caesium,' said Lars Eric de Geer, a radiologist at Sweden's Defence Research Institution. Three or four times before, the Swedes had identified reactor leaks of the same kind reaching their country – twice from unreported Soviet leaks. These had only been of a millionth of this intensity, however. The meteorologists tried to trace the air backwards, and found a line pointing across the Baltic, in the direction of the Black Sea. The Swedes began their own inquiries in Moscow. At lunchtime on Monday the Swedish technical and science attaché, Per Olof Sjostedt, contacted the Soviet State Committee for the Use of Atomic Energy but was told no information was available. At a Swedish embassy reception early on Monday evening, Swedish ambassador Torsten Orn inquired again, this time of a Soviet foreign ministry official, who simply took note of the request. No admission was made about Chernobyl.

Then at 9.02 p.m. the newscaster on the Moscow television news programme *Vremya* (*Time*) read a terse four-sentence statement from the Soviet Council of Ministers.

An accident has taken place at the Chernobyl power station, and one of the reactors was damaged. Measures are being taken to eliminate the consequences of the accident. Those affected by it are being given assistance. A Government Commission has been set up.

The Soviet hierarchy had made a policy decision not to provide any more details. The No. 2 man in the Swedish embassy, Lars-Ake Nilsson, requested additional information from a foreign ministry official, Yevgeny Rymko, who referred Nilsson to the official communiqué. 'I have no other information,' Rymko said.

The Soviet refusal to provide timely detail about the accident permitted two increasingly pervasive information-gathering organizations, the US intelligence community and the American media, to swing into frenzied action. For the first time in an international disaster of such a scale, the western media, with its huge resources for bringing instant information into the family living room, was totally without access to the action. The media's key source became, much as it was for western intelligence, spies in space – a new generation of civilian satellites which, in their ability to take detailed pictures, are rapidly catching up those belonging to the intelligence services. In fact, these new satellites have improved so much that the intelligence services view them, correctly, as their direct competition for information-gathering. The result, seen for the first time at Chernobyl, was a bizarre contest between the media and US intelligence trying to 'scoop' each other on the latest on the accident. It provided an extraordinary sideshow to

Chernobyl, a spectacle of modern electronic wizardry which lasted fully a week after the accident began and, in retrospect, badly distorted the true nature of the disaster.

President Reagan, travelling on an extended tour with top aides to Japan via various Pacific Islands, sat back in Air Force One as it hopped from one balmy spa to another and let it all happen, half the world away. At first, the President was personally detached, carefully avoiding the harsh anti-Soviet rhetoric of the past, and letting Gorbachev struggle with his own self-made public relations problem.

The United States has two types of spy satellites which have capabilities relevant to the Chernobyl accident. The first, codenamed MIDAS, the most secret of all the spy satellites currently in space, is primarily designed to detect the launch of a missile through the heat of its exhaust acting on the satellite's infra-red sensors. The first MIDAS satellites were tested in 1960, but the programme did not become operational until 1972. MIDAS, an acronym for Missile Alarm Detection System, was constantly updated with new satellites which, for security reasons, were always changing their identity. When defence officials went to Congress to ask for money for their secret project, MIDAS was programme 461 one year, than 266, then 949 and finally programme 647. For public consumption the money was allocated under the Defense Support Programme, or DSP. That is all the public knows. Here is how a State Department report to Congress describes DSP: '[Deleted] currently consists of [deleted] satellite – two [deleted] satellites – a [deleted] for [deleted] and the [deleted] satellites – and a [deleted] which provides a [deleted] for the [deleted].'

The DSP programme consists of three $150 million satellites parked 22,300 miles up in geosynchronous orbit: that is, they orbit the earth at precisely the same speed that the earth is revolving and thus always remain in the same spot. One is positioned over South America, another over the central Pacific, and a third over the Indian Ocean. They are 22 feet long, 9 feet in diameter and weigh 2,500 pounds. They maintain a constant watch over the Soviet Union, China and the oceans, and they are designed to provide the first warning of a missile attack, either by land or by sea.

Each satellite has an infra-red-detecting telescope, always pointing down to earth and set at an angle of 7.5 degrees from the body of the satellite. The telescope scans a conical area of the planet below as the satellite spins at a rate of seven turns a minute. A counter-motion wheel maintains stability. As long as there is no cloud cover of the earth's surface any infra-red energy within the conical field covered by the telescope is picked up and reflected off a mirror on to a series of 2,000 angled, two-dimensional detector cells made of lead sulphide, a compound highly sensitive to infra-red energy. The satellite computes data from the activated cells and is able to report the intensity of the infra-red energy and its point of origin on the earth's surface. Information from the satellite is then transmitted to two DSP 'readout stations', one in Colorado and one in Australia, where the data are processed and forwarded almost instantaneously to command posts on the American continent.

Within twenty-four hours of the Soviets admitting to the accident, a few well-informed American correspondents began asking the key question: had the DSP satellite been able to detect the explosion and fire at Chernobyl when it happened early on Saturday morning, 26 April, Moscow time? Larry Speakes, the White House press spokesman, travelling with the President, flatly denied that the United States knew anything about the accident before the Soviets made it public on the Monday evening, and, according to some independent intelligence analysts the DSP would probably *not* have picked up the intense heat source in the reactor.

There were intermittent clouds and rain showers over the reactor site during the weekend. At some time MIDAS would have had a clear view of the burning reactor containing temperatures of 3,000/4,000 °F. that are similar to those coming from the rocket of a nuclear missile. However, the analysts point out, it is not so much a matter of the temperature of the heat source as the size of it. DSP is calibrated to pick up the plume of a rocket motor that is a pillar of fire some 200 feet in diameter. Whether the reactor produced a sufficiently large heat source is still in doubt. Others say it could have been, and, therefore, probably was, discovered before the Soviets announced the accident. *Newsweek* reported that, '[Satellite] tapes recorded the previous Saturday showed infra-red images of a sudden flash in the vicinity of Kiev – apparently the explosion of the shattered reactor.'

If that is true, then what happened to this information is also a matter of speculation, but the best guess is that US intelligence analysts were somewhat bewildered: Chernobyl was not one of their primary targets for gathering intelligence. Their priority list would be missile silos and rocket test sites. Assuming, however, that a 'hot spot' at Chernobyl was recorded sometime over the weekend, US analysts would then try and discover more through other means, such as listening to normal telephone traffic and, if it was not already in place, by moving their one remaining reconnaissance satellite, the KH-11, over the site. The KH-11 is in polar orbit, passing over the same location about twice a day. It has small rocket motors that can push it over any spot in the world.

The KH-11 is a refinement of two earlier satellites, the KH-8 and the KH-9, both of which ceased operating in 1984. The KH-9 orbited roughly 100 miles above the earth's surface and was said to be able to photograph all of the Soviet Union and the People's Republic of China – or other nations of equivalent land mass – every three and a half days. Both satellites carried a variety of cameras and when the film had been exposed it was packed into canisters and parachuted back to earth where the canisters were either snagged by planes in mid-air or plucked out of the ocean by navy divers. The KH-11, by contrast, does not use film. Instead, it produces digital electronic impulses that are transmitted to other satellites and received almost immediately on the ground.

According to intelligence sources, the KH-11 took its first picture of Chernobyl on Monday, the same day as the Soviets made their official announcement of the accident – at 9 o'clock Monday evening. This suggests that the Americans either acted with amazing speed and were lucky to have the KH-11 close to the Chernobyl site, or that they knew, somehow, at least a few hours in advance of the official Soviet statement. In any event, the picture was not very helpful: one source said it was 'just a bunch of smoke'. Two more pictures were taken Tuesday morning and evening. The Tuesday evening picture was 'good and overhead', said the same source.

Based on the KH-11 information, US intelligence analysts began leaking a variety of interpretations of what was happening at Chernobyl to the American media. *Newsweek* reporters, for example, were told that when analysts looked at the pictures, 'They were astounded. The roof of the reactor had blown off and the walls were pushed out, like a barn collapsing in a high wind.' What startled analysts, however, was that the same set of pictures showed a barge peacefully sailing down the Pripyat river, as though nothing had happened. And, inside the plant fence, less than a mile from the burnt-out reactor, men could be seen, apparently playing soccer. An NBC TV news correspondent reported, the following day, Wednesday, that, 'Several congressmen said they were shown photos of the damaged plant, with a soccer game proceeding routinely only a few blocks away.'

The image was of a serious accident, getting worse, and being disregarded by an unsuspecting public. We now know that a mass evacuation of 40,000 inhabitants took place on Sunday, 27 April – and most independent analysts say the KH-11 should have been able to detect the ghost town left behind, but the Pentagon did not mention this. As the week progressed the flow of supposedly secret information from the National Reconnaissance Office (NRO), the headquarters of US covert satellite and aerial spying on the fourth floor of the Pentagon, astounded some analysts. 'They were out to toot their horn,' said one analyst. 'That KH-11 is the only one they have up there right now and people have been saying that, as a result, they're no good at collecting intelligence anymore. They wanted to prove they are good.' But the NRO was in a dilemma. They wanted to show they were good, but they could not show how good for two reasons: one technical and another political. First, they do not want the Soviets to know the technical capability of the KH-11. Second, and just as important, they have to deal with an administration that does not want to demonstrate that its intelligence monitoring system is capable of tricky detections and surveillance of this nature. The administration opposes arms control agreements with the Soviets on the basis that it cannot verify compliance with such agreements. The public disclosure of first-rate intelligence on the fire at Chernobyl could have diluted this argument.

Still, the NRO clearly felt the need to be visible. Their information was, for the first time during an international mass media event, in direct competition with a new generation of civilian satellites that are an open challenge from Europe to the United States monopoly of civilian satellite pictures. The challenge comes from SPOT, a French-owned satellite launched last February that offers much higher resolution than its older US competitor LANDSAT. SPOT, which stands for Système Probatoire d'Observation de la Terre, made its international début with a picture of Nice on the French Riviera including sharp details of the streets and marinas. Together these two satellites are revolutionizing western civilian information of the Soviet Union. US intelligence, which used to inhibit sales of what were considered sensitive LANDSAT pictures, has now been forced to abandon old security-conscious rules.

SPOT photos are marketed in the United States by a wholly-owned subsidiary of the French company, called SPOT Image Corporation, of Weston, Virginia. CIA director William Casey, who takes any opportunity he can to restrict press access to what he considers to be sensitive information, concedes that there is nothing the agency can do to stop news organizations, or private individuals, from buying pictures of military installations, either in the Soviet Union, the United States or anywhere else. 'I don't think there is anything we can do about it,' said Casey. 'Anybody can go out and get whatever information they can get, the press and anybody else in any other country . . . I expect that large news organizations will have one of those satellites themselves one of these days.'

In future, a situation could arise where news organizations just happen to have their satellites in a sensitive spot and at a particular time and, unwittingly, they become the possessors of sensitive intelligence that either the Americans or the Soviets do not want published. Gorbachev might call Reagan and say, 'Kill that TV programme, or no summit.' The legal implications for US news organizations are not clear. Casey warned recently that he considers the media have 'a responsibility to listen and consider' when the government argues that information should be withheld on national security grounds, a process that occurs even today.

But as far as is known, Chernobyl was of no great military

significance. The reactor was, apparently, employed solely for the production of electrical power – its existence was well known. The Soviets even boasted about it. The IAEA in Vienna had previously been invited to inspect it. US intelligence could not object to the media publishing whatever they could get their hands on. The problem for US intelligence was maintaining an image that they were better informed about the accident than the media – that their ageing KH-11 could not be 'scooped' by the cheeky new French SPOT.

Since 1972, the American civilian satellite LANDSAT has been selling pictures of the earth to farmers, oil companies, geologists, foresters, foreign governments and anyone else interested in land resource management. For prices between $50 and $3,300, depending on resolution, quality and location, anyone can have a picture of anywhere in the world. The smallest object, discernible by LANDSAT from about 400 miles up, is 98 feet square. The pictures are marketed by the Earth Observation Satellite Company (EOSAT), based in Lanham, Maryland, a joint venture of Hughes aircraft company and the RCA corporation. By contrast, SPOT's pictures are more expensive – $155 for a black-and-white print to $2,550 for a computer-compatible tape. But SPOT has a much improved capability: from 500 miles up it can pick out smaller objects down to 33 square feet. It also has another distinct advantage. It can view the same site more frequently than LANDSAT. While both satellites circle the globe in near polar orbits, LANDSAT covers nearly every location on earth in 16 days and SPOT takes 26. But LANDSAT's sensors look straight down, meaning that it can photograph a particular site only once every 16 days. SPOT's sensors look on either side of the satellite, allowing the same location to be viewed about twice a week. By viewing the same site from two angles, SPOT can also produce a three-dimensional effect.

On Tuesday, the fourth day of the accident, LANDSAT obtained the first photo of the Chernobyl plant. But before the LANDSAT picture could be made available to the TV networks, US intelligence had already managed to scoop it. Pentagon officials told the media they had already seen the first KH-11 reconnaissance pictures, taken late on Monday, showing the top of the reactor blown off and 'towering clouds of smoke that could endanger a second nuclear reactor nearby'. The pictures were so grim, the sources said, that they estimated thousands must have died. The same Pentagon sources told NBC that a report from United Press International, one of two American news wire services, saying that 2,000 had already died, 'seemed about right since 4,000 worked at the plant'.

The combination of the Pentagon's satellite intelligence and the UPI report made the situation look grave – and also made Moscow's official bulletin that evening look foolish. The bulletin said only two had died. The radiation leak had been stabilized, a town and three villages had been evacuated and other victims were getting medical attention. However, as far as can be told at the time of writing, the Moscow bulletin, though conservative, was accurate. The UPI estimate was a gross exaggeration, and the figure of the 2,000 dead topped all TV news programmes that Tuesday evening. UPI said the report came from a woman in Kiev, described by the news agency as someone with contacts in the Soviet rescue and health circles. The woman had said 80 people died immediately and 2,000 more died on the way to hospitals. A hospital in Kiev, the anonymous woman said, was 'packed with people who suffer from radiation sickness'. (Some other American news organizations treated the UPI report with considerable scepticism. The other US news agency (Associated Press) declined to carry the report. The *New York Times* separated the report from its main coverage of the accident and took the trouble to call the foreign editor of UPI to see if the news agency had been able to get any confirmation of the 2,000 figure, because no one else had. No, said foreign editor Sylvana Foa, adding, 'this source has never proved to be unreliable'.)

On Wednesday, the fifth day of the accident, two radio hams, one Dutch and one Israeli, fed the rumours of a second meltdown at the adjoining No. 3 reactor. In the northern Dutch town of Bergen, Annis Kofman was listening into short-wave transmission and reported that he picked up a conversation between a Soviet radio enthusiast in the Kiev region and a Japanese radio ham. According to the Russian, the accident 'certainly caused hundreds of deaths, perhaps, many, many more' and two reactors at the plant had been 'totally destroyed by a meltdown'. The message ended, 'the world has no idea of the catastrophe – help us'. The Israeli ham, quoted on NBC news, was reported to have talked to people who lived near Chernobyl. One crackly voice said, 'I saw . . . explosion of second reactor is very high . . . [sic] as of now we cannot . . . we are ordered to . . . all supplies we have.'

During Wednesday the view from Pentagon sources and from some unnamed administration officials was that the original reactor fire was getting much worse and that a second in the adjoining reactor was a possibility – a contradiction of the official Soviet bulletin that the main danger had passed. CBS news said that 'informed sources' had told them that detailed pictures taken by a US satellite showed Soviet aircraft circling the reactor building, apparently dumping chemicals on the still-burning fire. An administration official told them there could be a meltdown at the second reactor adjoining the one where the accident had occurred. Ian Rather, the CBS news anchor, summed up the day, 'A much different, much more dangerous view seen from western satellites above, enhanced eye-in-the-sky views that US intelligence says is a reactor-gone-wild accident still in progress and a second reactor possibly melting down.' The power of a network anchorman such as Rather cannot be underestimated. A recent poll showed that Americans believe his word above the President's.

In an effort to clear up the confusion, CBS news had obtained civilian LANDSAT satellite pictures from EOSAT, but, in fact, the pictures only created greater confusion. They were taken with an infra-red camera and, said CBS, 'appear to show two pinpoints of heat coming from the two reactors'. In its evening news show, NBC concluded that not only was the information flow confusing, the Pentagon itself was confused. 'You must remember,' said their correspondent, 'that this is the first time US intelligence experts have ever looked at pictures like these, so they're gonna make some mistakes.'

Indeed, in retrospect, they did err in their judgment – whether intentionally or not, only time will confirm. There was no second meltdown, not even a fire in the adjoining No. 3 reactor. The original fire was apparently brought under control when the Soviets said it had been. On Wednesday, however, this fact was confirmed, not by the Pentagon, but by SPOT. Its first picture of the site on Thursday morning, taken from 500 miles above the earth and released in Sweden, showed that smoke had stopped billowing from the reactor. It also showed a long dark scorch mark on the ground next to the reactor. The mark, at least 600 feet long, was believed to be the result of the blast. Smoke visible on the earlier LANDSAT photo, taken on Tuesday, had gone.

Still the Pentagon insisted that their high-resolution pictures, taken on Thursday morning by a US spy satellite, showed the fire was still burning. At the State Department, however, officials were more cautious. They declined to answer questions about whether the fire was out or not. This did not stop Secretary of State George Shultz from giving casualty estimates contradicting the Soviet figures. Moscow's official count, as of that Wednesday, was two dead, 197 injured, 18 of those seriously. 'Our own pictures give us information that suggests the casualty rates are higher than those that have been announced by the Soviet Union so far,' Shultz declared.

'So,' summed up ABC's Pentagon correspondent, John McWethy, 'after a week of monitoring the world's worst nuclear accident, American officials still don't know exactly what caused it or whether the fire that has burned so intensely for the last seven days is now finally out as the Soviets claim.'

The National Reconnaissance Office at the Pentagon had made its point: they had upstaged the civilian satellite information by contradicting it, had their own interpretation of the events broadcast by starved TV news organizations, and still managed to give nothing away about the exact nature of their own information or what they knew and when they knew it. None of their secret intelligence satellite pictures was ever seen by the public. In the end, the public were the losers on both sides of the Iron Curtain.

By the weekend the Soviets were clearly looking for a way to regain some of their tarnished public relations image – to show that, under Gorbachev, things could be different, that Soviet officials could be more forthcoming. They made a surprise appearance on Capitol Hill. For only the second time in the last fifteen years the Soviets sent an official from their Washington embassy to testify before congress. The diplomat chosen was Vitaly Churkin, a 34-year-old second secretary whose name appears No. 35 on the embassy diplomatic list but who has become known in Washington as the best public relations operative in the embassy. He is the resident expert on arms control and was broken into that trade as an interpreter at the Salt One talks. His neatly coiffured, prematurely grey hair, earnest good looks and quick wit put him firmly in the new Gorbachev mode, and he is a major figure on the cocktail, dinner and debate circuit. During his four years in Washington he has clearly won the confidence of his superiors and he is allowed to live with his wife outside the embassy compound. When asked by a reporter after his Capitol Hill appearance, whether he had been given instructions from Moscow to do so, Churkin said no, there had been no instructions. 'We are courageous fellows,' he quipped. Few believed him, and in fact, his appearance on Capitol Hill was arranged just an hour prior to a hearing before the House of Representatives Energy and Commerce Committee, which was meeting to discuss the implications of the accident for American nuclear power. Ed Markey, a young, liberal, anti-nuclear democrat from Massachusetts, called the Soviet Embassy at 10.30 a.m. on Thursday to say that Congress was concerned about the lack of Soviet disclosures and wanted to offer the embassy a chance to explain the Soviet position. Churkin appeared at 1.30 p.m.

In his testimony Churkin, for the most part, repeated the official Moscow line – the problem was 'being managed', the situation was 'improving', but 'unfortunately it was not yet all over with'. Speaking in good, idiomatic English, Churkin parried the barrage of critical questions: could Churkin tell the committee 'in layman's terms' why the accident happened, one Congressman wondered? 'Can you tell me in those same layman's terms why the *Challenger* disaster happened?' Churkin shot back. Could Churkin say whether radioactive material from the accident would damage Soviet grain production? In particular, would the accident force the Soviet Union to buy from the United States? 'Well, I understand that this question is not based entirely on humanistic grounds,' Churkin replied, drawing laughter from the crowd and an ackowledgment from Congressman Markey that 'we are in a capitalist country now'. His remark was a testament to the way communist secretiveness and capital jostling had combined to confuse and muddy a very dangerous situation for the planet.

7 The cloud spreads

'How technologically vulnerable the whole of modern civilization has become.'

Academician Georgiy Arbatov, *Pravda*, 9 May 1986

It was not the United States which faced the real dangers and problems of Chernobyl. The radioactivity from the exposed and blazing core of the reactor had shot high into the atmosphere, fuelled by hydrogen flames estimated to be up to 500 metres high. While the bulk of the heavy uranium and plutonium derivatives stayed in the reactor or fell locally, the rest – the lighter elements and gases – proceeded to drift for more than 1,500 km (1,000 miles), shedding their radioactive cargo on the wind, into the rain, and on to the fields of Europe.

Virtually every country in both eastern and western Europe was contaminated by radioactivity in the following week, some at potentially dangerous levels. Most was probably not harmful, although some people – such as pregnant women, babies, the weak and ill – were far more vulnerable than others. Furthermore, no one knew how much more radiation to expect from the inferno at Chernobyl. It was out of control and might continue to burn and radiate indefinitely. The reactor could well have exploded again if its core was not cooled and isolated.

The cloud had extraordinary consequences. It terrified millions of Europeans who found themselves gulping iodine solution; keeping their children indoors; not daring to buy lettuce, drink milk, go swimming, or let dust stay on their clothes. It was a sudden foretaste, perhaps, of the effects of a 'small' nuclear war in Europe.

Background radiation

To put the figures of radiation exposure from Chernobyl in context, it is helpful to summarize the doses normally experienced in everyday life, from natural and man-made sources. The figures apply to Britain, and come from the National Radiological Protection Board, but similar doses apply everywhere else.

Natural sources of radiation (the sun, the rocks in the earth, and radon gas of natural origin) produce an average annual dose of almost 200 millirems a year. In areas where natural radioactivity is higher – because of radioactive materials in rocks or building materials, or the build-up of radon caused by reduced ventilation – the average annual dose may be 300 mrem, with some individuals as high as 500 mrem.

Artificial sources add, on average, another 50 mrem a year, of which almost all comes from the medical use of X-rays. Some people, of course, will have no X-rays in the course of a year, so the 50 mrem figure is an average over the whole of the population. (A single chest X-ray gives the lung a dose of about 200 mrem.) Other man-made sources are fall-out from nuclear tests, discharge from power stations (0.3 mrem a year) and exposure at work.

So, perhaps, was the reaction of governments. Not all behaved in the same way. Some – predictably in parts of eastern Europe, but more strikingly in France –tried, for political reasons, to behave as if nothing had really happened. Others were understandably confused about what to do. This was not reassuring to their citizens: it appeared in some countries, notably Britain, that emergency plans were far from perfect.

It was also striking that many governments rapidly sensed political danger to their own nuclear power programmes. Ministers tried to reassure their electorates that: 'It couldn't happen here.' Their efforts were unsuccessful. The Soviet Union did its best to minimize the declared danger to foreign countries, although it gradually admitted that an appreciable roll-call of states had been affected.

At a Moscow press conference on 6 May, in answer to a written question from a Hungarian journalist on the effect of Chernobyl on other countries, Yuri Sedunov, first deputy chairman, USSR State Committee for Hydrometeorology and Environmental Control, said:

> In our opinion, there was no direct threat to the population either of our own areas which are far enough away ... or foreign countries. Certainly, the relevant services registered a rise in the natural background level of radiation. This was also noted by our radiation service.
>
> Because of the meteorological conditions, in the first few days, such a result did take place successively in a northerly direction, then north-west, then west, then south ... signs of enhanced radiation coming in waves were noticed in this succession in foreign countries.
>
> Up to 1 May, they were seen in Poland. After 2 May in Romania. We consider this plume was short-lived, not significant, not high-level. In comparison

with the background level, the rise was five times, according to measurements contiguous to the border (10 microrem per hour).

Polish radio, reporting the same press conference, was a little more specific:

> Sedunov ... said that under the effects of winds and air currents, some of the contaminated air mass ... passed over Poland, and also over Romania, Hungary and Yugoslavia. A higher degree of radiation was recorded in those states, but it did not present a danger to human health.

Tass reported the following day:

> A negligible portion of small radioactive particles was also distributed together with airflows over large distances and fell on the territory of Poland, Romania and of a number of Scandinavian countries. Here a slight increase in background radioactivity was observed, likewise not a danger to the population.

In reality, the situation was much worse.

Eastern Europe

The eastern bloc satellite countries were, after the hapless Russian territories of Belorussia and the Ukraine, the most badly affected. They suffered involuntary irradiation, secrecy, and economic damage.

On 10 May, the European Community finally decided to ban the import of fresh food for the remainder of May from the Soviet Union, Poland, Czechoslovakia, Hungary, Bulgaria and Yugoslavia. East Germany, although it was just as vulnerable to radioactive contamination, was mysteriously omitted from the list at the insistence of West Germany, which values its trading links with its eastern counterpart. This was done on the grounds that it was beyond a '1,000 km limit' around Chernobyl. Austria, on the other hand, as a western country, escaped although it was partly inside the 1,000 km limit.

There was an outcry against the ban in the Comecon countries, as beef, fruit and even snails piled up in railway sidings: it was undoubtedly confused and inconsistent. The ban was also to the commercial advantage of European farmers. It is estimated to have cost the eastern bloc $975 million in lost exports, most of them not from the USSR, but from the unfortunate eastern European satellites.

Poland was the first foreign country across whose borders the radioactive cloud actually blew. As the most disaffected of the eastern European satellites, it was ironic that Poland got the worst and most rapid dose. The Polish authorities were irrevocably committed to a programme of nuclear expansion. Their very first nuclear power plant was being built at Zarnowiec on the Baltic coast opposite Sweden and close to the border with the Soviet Union. A second plant was planned for Wloclawek.

In western Poland, at Lubusz, a site for a nuclear waste dump in the 1990s had just been designated. The underlying popular fear of nuclear dangers had been demonstrated there in a remakable fashion only weeks earlier. The official local radio station reported that local opinion was 'outraged' by the plan for a dump.

Members of the Sejm, the parliament, were immediately sent to hold talks with local officials and that gesture of nervousness was, too, officially reported. Only the previous year, the academic council of the Institute of Nuclear Chemistry had reported that far too few radiation safety experts were being trained in the country, and said the situation was so disastrous that the very survival of radiological protection was in jeopardy. A week after the accident, the underground organization Kos put out a cyclostyled information sheet which summarized local events with some apparent accuracy. It said:

What Happened and What is to be done?
The facts known to us about the radioactive danger to Poland.

The most powerful radioactive cloud arrived over Poland on Monday 28 April. Officially, the highest degree of radiation was registered at Mikolajki. It reached 2.5 mrem per hour – over 200 times higher than the background level of radiation. This information was given at the press conference for foreign journalists on 1 May. The deputy director of the central laboratory for radiological protection, Jaworewski, declared that information to the population had been deliberately delayed in order to give it at a moment when the prophylactic action had already been undertaken, and in this way, panic had been avoided such as that which accompanied the accident at Three Mile Island.

The cloud must have been very extensive. For on the same day, there was even consideration of switching off the reactor at Swierk where a rise of 10 times in radiation was recorded in the area of the research establishment.

News about the accident had not yet reached Poland. Within 50 km of the area with the greatest radioactive figures, are found the towns of Byalistock, Olstin, Elblag, Gdansk, Gdynia and Sopot. At 200–250 km, apart from Warsaw, are Plock, Torun, Bydgoscz, Koszalin, Stettin. Even further, but still within the area of fall-out are Lodz, Poznan and Gorzow.

HOW THE RADIATION SPREAD

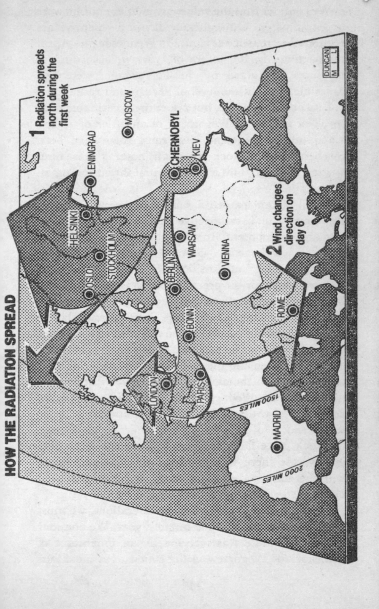

1 Radiation spreads north during the first week

2 Wind changes direction on day 6

MOSCOW

LENINGRAD

CHERNOBYL

KIEV

HELSINKI

STOCKHOLM

OSLO

WARSAW

VIENNA

BERLIN

BONN

LONDON

PARIS

ROME

MADRID

1500 MILES

2000 MILES

DUNCAN MIL

We consider that the values given to the public were underestimated. On that same day in Sweden, values registered were twice as high. On Wednesday 30 April, radioactivity in the centre of Warsaw, according to measures conducted by the Polytechnic, were 150 times higher than the level of background radiation.

Reasonably reliable, but not entirely verifiable data speak of a peak **at** Wegorzew, of an order of 1,500–1,700 times. The same level must then have been reached at Byalistock although nothing has been written about it. This is a substantial threat to human health.

A fall of rain caused a raising by several times of the already high radioactive level in the immediate human environment. In the following days, further waves of radioactive fall-out came over Poland, heading in different directions, of lesser intensity. At that moment, for all practical purposes, the whole of Poland was being affected by radioactive substances.

During the night of Mondáy–Tuesday, ambulances supplied a flow of Lugol (iodine solution) to the homes of members of the nomenklatura – the party and state elite. The police and the secret police carried out their own action for themselves. The general distribution took place on Wednesday morning. The supply of Lugol, given with a spoon without dilution can create severe shock to children with a tendency to allergy: this took place fairly frequently in the schools where in any case there were too few anti-histamine drugs and the state of health of many children has been unsatisfactory and disturbing for some time.

. . . if we wish to avoid genetic alterations, we must avoid radiation above 500 mrem a year. We consider that such a dose was received by an inhabitant of Byalistock or Wegorzew in the course of at most four days. And it is probable that it took place in the course of a single day. A dose three times bigger, of 1,500 mrem, possibly received instantaneously, is possibly even more dangerous. A dose of 3,000 mrem received in a short time is blatantly damaging to the health. If that were to happen, the excess over the background levels of radiation must reach a level of 30,000 times – values of this level were not recorded anywhere in Poland.

Thus, direct damage by radiation to human health of adults will not occur. But we should remember that the damage and the accumulation of iodine-131 [and other substances] ... could have worse effects on children. Thus in the future there await us less visible but long-term consequences – a weakening of the health of children, very possibly increases in cancers and mutations – but this is merely guesswork because we do not have the necessary data. A gigantic experiment has been carried out on us, and the entire world will now watch with the greatest interest to see what happens to these laboratory rabbits. . . .

At present it would be wrong to eat fresh greens which have been growing in the fields. Only long washing can partly reduce the threat. Safer are tomatoes and cucumbers and other green vegetables grown under glass. As time passes, the threats will begin to preponderate from the absorption of radioactivity into growing things and animals. Strawberries and cherries are the first fruits and they may well be the most threatened and damaged. It would be safer to use bottled strawberries prepared in winter, or autumn fruits. Milk will not be distributed for public use probably for at least 2 months. Almost certainly, however, the peasants are going to use this milk to feed their pigs, which means that pork and pork products will constitute a threat to health between May and August. Country chickens and especially village eggs will be less good for the health than those from poultry farms. It is decidedly not a good idea to eat Baltic fish, because of their iodine content, until the end of the year. The continuous dosage of Lugol is at present at best useless, and can be damaging to health. . . .

Clearly, the thing was not possible to conceal in the west for very long – nor in Poland, where people listen to foreign radio programmes, and the underground was able to expose the existing situation and inform society about it. And yet here it was attempted to keep silent as long as possible. This led to the result that the preventive measures were taken at least one day too late. . . .

Our local enthusiasts for nuclear energy have adopted absolutely typical attitudes. On the one side they try to pooh-pooh the scale of the tragedy. On the other, they assure us that we, at least, have got proper protection. In the west, they build a power station with a double jacket of ferro-concrete. These people here are proposing at Zarnowiec a 'half-jacket' – whatever that is supposed to mean. Gdynia-Gdansk is only 50 km away in the direction of the prevailing winds. . . .

So, there you are. In the Ukraine an enormous tragedy; in the whole of Europe an ecological catastrophe. What is happening in Moscow, which is responsible for it?

Well, in Moscow, they're having a parade. . . .

A 'Green' movement had flourished in Poland during the days of the Solidarity anti-government campaign five years earlier. One of its major successes, for example, had been to force the closure of the notorious Skawina steelworks in south-east Poland, whose emissions were seriously damaging to people's health.

On this occasion, the underground also reported:

> On 2 May in Wroclaw, a few dozen of the Freedom and Peace movement carried out a demonstration in connection with the ecological catastrophe at Chernobyl. They protested against the blockade of information about the course and the results of the catastrophe and the rejection by Soviet authorities of offers of help from the west to extinguish the fire. There was raised the cry: 'Zarnowiec will be the next!' and 'The threat is growing'. A number of groups of passers-by joined the demonstration and several hundred people gathered nearby. After the demonstration, the police arrested five persons.

Within a fortnight, the signatures of 300 Poles to a protest petition in Byalistock were handed to western reporters. They called for a halt to the Zarnoviec nuclear plant until the International Atomic Energy Agency (IAEA) was allowed to supervise the project.

Immediately after the accident, East Germany merely announced that there was no danger to the population from the mishap. It provided no details on radiation levels. East Germany has an ambitious nuclear power programme, with seven reactors built and another eight planned. 'It's difficult to organize any independent initiatives here,' said one human rights activist. But another young Lutheran pastor pointed to the intertwining of Europe which makes it impossible to seal off one country's folly from another. 'At the end of the day,' he said, 'we simply switch on West German television.'

In Czechoslovakia, repeated reports had emerged in the

west of expensive delays and malfunctions in the country's Bohunice nuclear plant – one of six near Austria and Hungary's borders. The remains of the Charter 77 dissident group issued statements condemning the lack of nuclear safety as the Chernobyl cloud arrived. The sale of milk was prohibited as the cloud veered over the country's mountains. However, senior Czech officials told the *Observer* that the milk was merely being stored. When the level of radioactivity was considered to have decayed sufficiently, it would be quietly used up.

Like all the Comecon countries, Hungary was well aware of the subterranean fear of nuclear energy among her people. It has a single medium-sized Soviet PWR power station at Paks in the middle of the country, with three reactors operating and a fourth being built. During its construction seven years ago, the Hungarian government went out of its way to stress the safety factors incorporated there.

The arrival of the Chernobyl cloud demonstrated abruptly what harm a reactor accident in central Europe can do to the countries around it, whether from the eastern bloc or the west. First there was suspicion and fear among the populace. 'We were told at first that nothing was wrong,' said one Budapest mother. 'Then they say, "Take precautions . . . wash fruit and vegetables." Either there is a problem or there isn't.'

A frustrated Hungarian TV reporter, Mihaly Hardi, filed a live report from Moscow on 29 April, in which he said: 'I tried all day to get information . . . but so far I have been told nothing.' A Central Committee official, Dr Matyas Szuroes, said on Budapest radio, 'Every individual has the right to more information and open dialogue.' He went on: 'We do support scientific progress, but we must take into account people's anxieties about an incident like this.'

The Hungarian authorities insisted – predictably – that Hungarian food had not been contaminated by fall-out. The

World Health Organization agreed. Senior foreign trade ministry official Tibor Antalpeter claims: 'We did everything possible to monitor our radioactivity levels. We gave the European Community daily data reports on the measures we were taking; we even said we would guarantee every product leaving the country and certify the food was safe.' But large numbers of Hungarians simply stopped buying fresh food. A pregnant Budapest wife, Agnus Csongar, explained in mid-May that she had not eaten any fresh meat, fruit, vegetables, cream or yoghurt for nearly two weeks. She, her husband, and six-year-old daughter were living on tinned meat and frozen vegetables. 'I don't want to take any risks,' she said straightforwardly: 'Now that I am pregnant, I have to be even more careful.'

At the same time, western Europe included Hungary in its hasty ban on food imports until the end of May: agricultural products make up more than 20 per cent of Hungary's foreign trade warnings, and this second blow to Hungary's farmers caused great bitterness. Antalpeter protested in the official daily *Magyar Hirlap* that it was 'completely political ... totally unjust and discriminatory ... It's an unjust decision.' It would have been no consolation had the Europeans chorused back at him the words of the ordinary housewife in Budapest: 'I don't want to take any risks.'

By 13 May, Yugoslavia allowed milk and dairy products to be consumed again, but ordered fruit and vegetables to be washed before eating. They remained hit by the ban on exporting milk and vegetables to western Europe. The previous week, Yugoslavia suddenly dropped all plans to build a second nuclear reactor at Prevlaka near Zagreb to accompany their PWR at Krsko, near Italy and Austria. This decision was accompanied by an environmental protest rally in the north-western city of Ljudljana, where about 1,000 young men gathered to urge a, no doubt sympathetic, government to seek compensation from the Soviet Union for radiation damage from Chernobyl.

Romania instituted health precautions as soon as the Soviet Union gave details of the accident. It was one of the first countries to be irradiated when the wind made a shift of direction from north to south. But they did not up-date radiation readings, merely saying a week later that radioactivity had decreased in some areas, but remained high in others. Romania has two reactors on the side of the country nearest the Black Sea – at Olt and Cernovoda. It plans to build three more on the same sites.

All the east European governments, however much they tried not to alarm their populaces, were deeply upset by Chernobyl. By the middle of May, authoritative sources told the *Observer*, unpublicized plans were being made for a 'summit' at Budapest to discuss the effects on them all of the catastrophe.

Scandinavia

Finland has two nuclear power stations, bought from Russia, on the Baltic coast facing Sweden and the Soviet Union. They are at Loviisa and Olkiluoto. Due to enter service in 1978, Loviisa was delayed because the Finns were not prepared, on safety grounds, to accept a Soviet pressurized water reactor without a 'secondary containment'. This is required in the west, but not installed in the Soviet Union. (The PWR is a different type from the Chernobyl reactor.) Finland also insisted on re-engineering the Soviet-made sensor and control systems. The Soviet reactor has apparently worked well: ironically, it was the containment dome ordered from the US Westinghouse corporation which developed awkward faults in the slag seals of its corrosion-resistant coating. After Chernobyl, Finland said it would postpone a decision on whether to build a planned fifth reactor for its two sites.

Official reaction in parts of the west to Chernobyl may have been muted — or worse — for fear of a backlash against the local nuclear power lobby. In Finland, information about the accident was muted, for two reasons. Civil servants had been on strike for almost a month when the accident happened, and most did not return for at least a week after it. This undoubtedly reduced the flow of information, though the levels of radiation were being monitored by Finnish scientists, who produced a series of reports. In addition, Finland has a long tradition of reticence where the Soviet Union is concerned.

It could be argued — as some Finnish journalists did — that it was best to avoid the kind of sensationalism which filled the pages of the US press with stories of mounds of non-existent Soviet corpses. But there was more to it than that. When the home affairs minister Kaisa Raatikainen was questioned on the lack of information about Chernobyl and its effect on Finland, she said tersely: 'There is no reason to inform. It will only create anxiety.' Finland was the only Nordic country not to join in a call to the Soviet authorities for more information on Chernobyl.

This kind of behaviour is called 'Finlandization' in the rest of Europe. It means that democratic attitudes towards press freedom are carefully altered to cope with the presence of a large Soviet neighbour on her borders. One frustrated editor said in mid-May: 'There were hopes that we were moving away from this kind of thing. This ultra-cautious attitude gives the impression of Finland as a land that keeps its mouth shut rather than speaks freely.'

But one of the main anxieties was that Finnish TV newscasts can be easily picked up in Soviet Estonia, where they are understandable to the locally born population. That might well have led to Soviet protests. The Baltic states of Estonia and Lithuania had previously shown enough resentment about nuclear power to deter the Soviet Union from forcing through its full construction programme there.

Finland's reports on the radioactive fall-out from the Chernobyl cloud raised questions. Local radiation levels were orginally reported as being the highest in the Nordic area immediately after Chernobyl exploded. At a post-Chernobyl Nordic crisis meeting in Stockholm two weeks later, the radiation experts from Helsinki surprised the Swedes by claiming that the highest amount of iodine-131 found in Finnish milk was 50 becquerels. Some samples in neighbouring Sweden were much higher.

Whatever the officials said, it was none the less reported that Finns were warning their children not to pick up dead migratory birds. They might have flown north from Russia.

The Lapps of the far north probably did worst in Scandinavia because of the Chernobyl cloud, according to studies by the Oslo Institute for Radiological Hygiene. The nomadic tribesmen are already estimated to have ingested 15–30 times as much radiation as other Norwegians, thanks to the atmospheric nuclear tests of the 1950s and 1960s. The Institute monitors radiation in their staple diet – which is reindeer meat.

About 80 per cent of the radioactive fall-out that fell in Sweden dispersed within a week. The rest drained through the watercourses into rivers and lakes. Fresh snow and rain four days after the accident in northern Sweden was 10 times above normal level.

Eventually, the Swedes discovered tiny particles of plutonium in the rainwater falling on their east coast. It was only 20 per cent above normal level, and not apparently from weapons-grade plutonium, but it demonstrated that the bowels of the reactor core had been involved in the burn-up.

Stockholm scientists said on 16 May that up to 20 delayed cancers might appear in Sweden over the next 40 years. Although radiation levels were falling, food restrictions would remain for several weeks.

The Swedish premier, Ingvar Carlsson, moved to strengthen Sweden's existing commitment to phase out nuclear power in 25 years. He said that if the commission investigating the Chernobyl accident found Swedish plants to be unsafe, some could be shut down even earlier.

A small country with no nuclear power stations of her own, Denmark immediately protested at the failure of the Soviet Union to provide information, and said she would seek a nuclear accidents treaty with her neighbours. The worst of the first cloud missed Denmark, although it was a Danish truck which was one of the first to arrive in the west having driven through the Kiev region. It had 50 times normal radiation on its body and tyres.

People started to queue to buy iodine tablets in Copenhagen.

Western Europe

In Germany, it was only on the night of Tuesday 29 April – nearly four days after the explosion – that the Soviet ambassador Yuli Kvitzinski officially told Friedrich Zimmerman, the West German interior minister, that the Chernobyl reactor had been damaged. The other three reactors on the site, although undamaged, had been shut down as a security precaution, he said. Before going to see Zimmerman, the Soviet ambassador went to the Bonn foreign ministry with a more urgent question for the panic-striken emergency team in Moscow. Who was there in Germany who knew how to extinguish a graphite fire? One of his colleagues then went to the German AtomForum headquarters – the association of all German nuclear users – and asked the same question. There were few answers: 'No one has that experience,' the AtomForum spokesman said: 'No one thought a graphite core could ignite.' Kvitzinski told the West German government that an unspecified amount of radioactive material had been released into the atmosphere at Chernobyl and the populace had been evacuated 'from the immediate area'. He attempted to assure the German minister that the situation was 'now under control'. Zimmerman renewed Bonn's offer of 'whatever help we can give', but he also demanded more information. Chancellor Kohl was to write to Gorbachev offering to call a global conference in Bonn on future nuclear policy.

It was immediately obvious that Chernobyl would threaten the future of the German nuclear power industry as well as the health of its citizens; Heinz Riesenhuber, the Bonn technology minister, countered the immediate – and predictable – demand from the Green Party that all German nuclear plants should be closed, by saying no such accident could happen in West Germany. The safety precautions were, he said reassuringly, much more stringent. What Chernobyl demonstrated, according to him, was the need for an effective international nuclear safety and control organization. As he spoke, radioactivity from Chernobyl showed up as double the normal measurements from air monitors in West Berlin and Bavaria. Experts rapidly announced that this presented no health danger to Germans. But some state governments closed swimming-pools and children's play areas; cancelled sports events; and told parents to bathe their children if they played outside. Varying limits on radioactivity were imposed on milk-processing plants, and some areas banned the harvesting of lettuces and chives grown out of doors. The federal government had to promise 'speedy help' to farmers facing the prospect of milk poured away and cattle unable to eat grass in the fields rather than costly fodder.

The interior minister, Zimmerman, eventually made an angry TV broadcast. The government had recommended precautions only because of the uncertainty about Chernobyl, he said, and the wisdom of minimizing any long-term hazards. He accused some state governments of causing 'hysteria and confusion' by their over-zealousness.

Zimmerman and his colleagues were unable to return, however, to politics as usual. On Sunday 18 May a group of protesters bombarded police guarding a nuclear waste treatment centre at Wackersdorf. They hurled petrol bombs, fireworks and stones at them.

In the wake of the Chernobyl cloud, the ruling Christian Democratic Union of Chancellor Helmut Kohl stuck staunchly to the party's pro-nuclear stance. But there were signs of wavering. The chairman of the biggest of the state parties, Kurt Biedenkopf of North Rhine-Westphalia, regarded as one of the CDU's progressive thinkers, began to move some way towards the idea of nuclear power only being a 'transitional option'. Chernobyl immediately became a live issue in regional elections due in June in Lower Saxony. With the appearance of the Chernobyl cloud, opinion polls gave the opposition Greens and the Social Democrats (the SPD) a majority together over the governing party. The SPD offered to close down all local nuclear plants which could not pass stringent new safety inspections: the Greens held out for more.

Austria's would-be entry into the nuclear power club had been abruptly halted seven years earlier, and a large boiling-water reactor at Zwentendorf has since stood mothballed near the Czech border, as a testament to popular hostility. The Socialist Party then in government, had felt sufficiently confident to build the reactor before holding a promised referendum in 1979. The referendum voted against atomic energy. Since then the government, of which the Socialists were now the main coalition partner, had been seeking to find an excuse to hold a new referendum in the hope of reversing the anti-nuclear decision and finally opening Zwentendorf.

Chernobyl changed all that. Environment became the key issue in the pending Austrian presidential elections. There was already growing uneasiness about two of Czechoslovakia's four nuclear reactor sites, whose possible danger-zone similarly straddles the Austrian border, and which had a history of accidents and stoppages.

After Chernobyl, the Czechs gave Austrian TV unprecedented freedom to film inside the Czech reactors, and stressed that they were not the same water-cooled graphite type as that at Chernobyl. But the Conservative favourite in the presidential elections, Kurt Waldheim, and his Socialist opponent, Kurt Styrer, both called for Zwentendorf to be dismantled. The Socialist politicans who had been previously energetic members of the nuclear energy lobby, changed their minds. 'The power station is dead and buried,' one said.

In Italy, the strength of anti-nuclear feeling was demonstrated when an estimated 100,000 people marched in protest through Rome calling for a ban on nuclear power, with the backing of left-wing parties.

The anti-nuclear movement in Italy had been only moderately strong, and elements in the powerful Communist party were prepared to back a modest nuclear programme.

But as sales of milk and leafy vegetables were restricted in Sicily and Sardinia, the local authorities at Trino Vercellese, in Piedment, asked the electricity organization to stop preparing a site for a nearby plant. They demanded a 'pause for reflection' until new safety standards could be established. The Italian government insisted that Italy's nuclear plans would go ahead, to add at least three plants to the country's existing four.

But when the Socialist Party, one of the Craxi government's five coalition partners, called for the elderly Latina plant, south of Rome, to be closed down immediately, there was rapid pressure from Britain. The British electricity authorities urged Italy not to yield to it The plant, built in the 1950s without advanced safety features, was in any event due to be phased out. But it is a Magnox plant: and Britain feared that such an event could lead to similar pressure to shut the UK's own nine Magnox plants. The industry saw Chernobyl, once again, as a threat to itself.

After ten days, Dutch radiation was back to normal, officials said, although overnight rain had doubled background radiation in soil levels. But Dutch nuclear policy had not returned to normal. Holland has two nuclear plants operating, Borssele and Dodewaard, near the Channel coast and the German border respectively. Chernobyl immediately forced the suspension of plans for a major nuclear expansion in the 1990s; the centre-right government was facing elections and a Labour Party with a popular anti-nuclear stance.

Switzerland, size for size, is now one of the biggest nuclear nations in the world. They have four reactors built at Muhleberg, Gosgen-Daniken, Beznau and Liebstadt, and another two planned, at Kaiseraugst and Graben. They plan to generate 30 per cent of their power from nuclear energy.

A week after the disaster, drinking rainwater was still banned in Switzerland, and pregnant women and children under two were warned not to drink milk. Radiation levels were 10 times above normal in the southern canton of Ticino. The government said there was no danger to public health. But a fortnight later, farmers in Berne were advised to reduce feeding of green fodder to livestock. Meat samples revealed radioactive traces of the metal caesium. These were 'above the maximum' set for imported meat in the wake of Chernobyl. Federal commission monitoring fall-out said meat radiation levels were expected to rise further in the immediate future. The commission spokesman, Ulrich Imobersteg, said they also recommended delaying slaughter, because the radioactivity decayed more quickly in live animals. But a slaughter ban was not planned.

In France, the first reaction to the news of Chernobyl came from a spokesman for Electricité de France who claimed that safety precautions at the 51 French nuclear plants were better than those of the Russians.

On one side of a Rhine bridge, at Kehl, in West Germany, the children were forbidden to play on the grass and the lettuces sat uneaten in the ground. On the French side of the bridge, around Strasbourg, very similar lettuces were declared harmless. The reluctance of the French government to divulge any knowledge of the Soviet disaster or to admit any concern about contamination, led to sharp comment in the French press. The daily *Liberation* wrote that France was 'the most nuclearized country in Europe', where anti-nuclear opposition had evaporated. Yet the authorities 'hide with exemplary firmness behind their wall of silence'. One French ecologist said sarcastically that the fall-out cloud which covered the rest of Europe seemed to have decided to omit France from its itinerary. 'Perhaps it has been like the US attack on Libya: our government simply refused to allow the cloud into our airspace.'

Eventually, the French were forced to admit that they had detected radioactivity up to 400 times higher than background, but had been concealing it. On 16 May, the government belatedly set up a free telephone hotline for citizens. By the end of the month, France found itself admitting that an accident had just occurred at their Cap de la Hague reprocessing plant, on the Channel coast facing the UK. Five workers had received doses over the safety limit, up to 18 rem. The French government was also forced to admit that a near-catastrophic accident had occurred, but had been concealed, in 1984, in one of their supposedly 'safe' nuclear plants at Bugey, near the Swiss border. It seemed that even French insouciance was beginning to crack beneath the cloud of Chernobyl.

Great Britain

On Friday, 2 May, the radioactive cloud from Chernobyl finally, inevitably, reached Britain. First official reports were cautious and reassuring. The Meteorological Office at Bracknell in Berkshire announced that the cloud would merely 'clip the corner of Kent and then pass over the eastern part of East Anglia before being blown northwards out into the North Sea'. Dr Donald Acheson, chief medical officer at the Department of Health, added that there would be no risk to the public.

In keeping with past traditions of issuing calm assurances, doing little lest the public become 'over-concerned' and of attempting to maintain the nuclear industry in the best possible light, the government reacted with sluggishness.

By Monday, 6 May, as the radioactive cloud moved towards south-west England, householders in Scotland and Wales who drank rainwater were being advised to limit their intakes. Government officials claimed that despite such 'outside precautions' radiation levels over Britain remained extremely low and were no threat.

But it quickly became apparent that the government was confused and ill-prepared – even though it had known about the Chernobyl disaster for a week. For instance, 'safe' figures issued by the Ministry of Agriculture were later discovered to diverge markedly from figures given out by the Scottish

Office, the department responsible for the region, which had found radioactivity of 440 becquerels a litre in milk, almost half the IAEA's stated danger level for children.

The revelation led Scottish National Party chairman Gordon Wilson to accuse the government of 'Kremlin style' secrecy. Such remarks had an element of political opportunism in them, of course. Much more revealing was the reaction of senior Conservative backbencher Sir Richard Body, a normally reliable supporter of the government, who accused it of having been caught 'completely off guard' by the passing of the cloud. For their part, opposition Labour MPs attempted – unsuccessfully – to have an emergency Commons debate held over the 'inadequate' provision of public information.

Attempts by Environment Minister, Kenneth Baker, to defuse the situation – by issuing assurances that radiation was 'nowhere near the levels at which there is any hazard to health' – were not helped by John Dunster, head of the National Radiological Protection Board (NRPB), who announced that the board's calculations showed that there would be 'a few tens' of UK cancer deaths over the next 50 years as a result of the Chernobyl cloud.

Public confusion and alarm only deepened when it was discovered that the government's reassuring figures – which showed that iodine-131 levels in milk measured only 60 becquerels a litre – contrasted with the independent NRPB's figures that revealed that levels were as high as 390 in Scotland, 350 in Northern Ireland and 370 in Cumbria – areas that had all experienced heavy rainfall in previous days. (The IAEA's stated safe level for children is 1,000.)

By Tuesday, 7 May, it was clear that Whitehall was in a state of considerable confusion as to responsibility for the provision of facts to a now very distressed public. The Ministry of Agriculture and the National Water Council passed inquiries to the Department of the Environment which in turn passed them on to bemused officials of the Departments of Health and Energy. Emergency phone numbers that were issued were permanently engaged.

Eventually, one minister – Mr Baker – was given the role of co-ordinating public information. Even then the confusion continued. One Department of the Environment scientist who was contacted by *The Times* said he could only provide information to the public – not to the press.

By this time much of the British public was in a thorough state of alarm. The prospect of a deadly but invisible killer that had spread across the country – ironically over a Bank Holiday, a time of traditional outdoor activity – began to trigger some odd reactions. For instance, the £3,000-a-year Dulwich College preparatory school in Kent demanded that all local milk supplies come from cows that had been fed indoors on 'nuclear-free' silage!

Then, on Thursday, 8 May, the government announced it had finally got its official response programme in full swing. It issued special emergency telephone numbers for anxious members of the public. Those who used them got some curious replies, however. Instead of hearing the reassuring tones of a well-informed civil servant, some callers were routed through to the drivers' rest-room at the Department of the Environment. It was a farcical climax to an already chaotic week.

The Chernobyl cloud – by the time it reached Britain – was a relatively weakened beast. Compared with a plume that would pour across the United Kingdom from a stricken British reactor (or from one in a neighbouring country such as France), it was a minor threat to public health. But Britain's official response proved to be so woefully inadequate, it merely inflamed public disquiet.

Environment groups such as Friends of the Earth and

Greenpeace had a field day. Manned by articulate, efficient and committed spokesmen, their switchboards were swamped by tidal waves of calls. Sometimes, the environmentalists even found themselves in the unlikely position of giving out reassuring advice on the government's behalf.

In all, the passage of the Chernobyl cloud was a public relations disaster for the government. Its civil nuclear disaster preparations were shown to be quite inadequate. The situation was summed up by Newcastle University geographer Stanley Openshaw, author of *Nuclear Power: Siting and Safety*: 'The government's plans are based on a gamble – a gamble that there won't be a major nuclear accident. That is just not viable.'

Public fears about the Chernobyl cloud triggered renewed scrutiny of emergency plans for dealing with a UK nuclear plant disaster. It was not a comforting experience. According to government plans, a serious nuclear accident would be followed by the prompt evacuation of named inhabitants living within 2.4 km (1.5 miles) of a nuclear plant. Yet at Chernobyl, Soviet authorities were forced to move people living within 30 km (19 miles) of the stricken reactor. In America, the statutory evacuation zone is 16 km (10 miles). In Sweden 40 to 80 km (25 to 50 miles) is considered necessary.

In defence of these plans, the Central Electricity Generating Board said evacuation zones could be enlarged if necessary – though the names of local inhabitants would not be known to the police (who would be in charge of the evacuation) within these enlarged areas. Dr Openshaw believes such arguments are completely inadequate:

If Britain had an accident like Chernobyl, we would have to evacuate people within 30 km (19 miles) of the affected nuclear plant. That would be impossible.

Around reactors like those at Berkeley, Oldbury, and Hartlepool, there are almost one million local inhabitants – in each case. If you tried to evacuate people from the area, you would also generate incredible panic and would jam roads within minutes. You just could not get people out.

Plans for dealing with contaminated food were shown to be equally inadequate. After a serious UK nuclear accident, agriculture ministry officials believe there would be no risk to milk supplies beyond 40 km (25 miles) of a damaged reactor. A ministry nuclear emergency plan even states: 'It is most unlikely that the risk could extend that far.' Yet after Chernobyl, milk was banned as far away as 1,280-km (800-mile) distant Sweden and 640-km (400-mile) distant Poland.

Other British measures were shown merely to be comic. The agriculture ministry stipulates that officials at its emergency operations centre will require sufficient supplies of headed notepaper, kettles and crockery 'for use outside of normal office hours'. In addition electricity board plans reassure staff that there are 'comprehensive stocks of equipment for emergency use'. The list opens: Wellington boots, 500 pairs' and is dominated by other emergency items such as household gloves, cotton caps and white coats. Far more chilling are preparations for medical care. At Sizewell, in Suffolk – where the electricity board wants to build Britain's first PWR plant beside its present ageing Magnox station – emergency plans state that injured and contaminated people would be taken to nearby Ipswich hospital for treatment. Yet doctors there have warned that they could deal with only four or five victims at a time. 'Any more than that and we would have to stack them up outside,' said Dr Michael Bush, assistant medical officer for East Suffolk.

Given the impact of a major disaster at Sizewell (the former Greater London Council estimated that 24,000 Londoners would contract fatal cancers, 3,500,000 would have to be evacuated from the city, and 615 sq. km (240 square miles) of the capital could be laid waste by a radioactive cloud pouring from Sizewell), the effectiveness of the government's response to the moderate problem of the Chernobyl cloud is extremely worrying. This view is shared by the government's own scientists. The annual meeting of the Institution of Professional Civil Servants, government scientists' main union in Britain, in mid-May condemned the government's slow and inefficient response to Chernobyl. One meteorologist, Peter Taylor, said the government had taken ten days to release figures that showed that parts of Scotland had been badly contaminated and that the public still did not know the exact locations of the worst effected areas. Other delegates criticized the government for setting 'safe' radiation dose levels that were five times higher than those suggested by the International Commission for Radiological Protection.

In a country which takes pride in its capacity to respond to emergencies, boasts of its democratic provision of public information, and continually proclaims its civil nuclear sophistication, the passage of the Chernobyl cloud over Britain proved to be a humiliating experience.

The United States

In the United States itself, where there were no fears from the distant European fall-out, the wilder claims about widespread Russian disaster eventually began to abate.

On Capitol Hill, Kenneth Adelman, the arms control administrator and unquestioning conduit for administration policy, had originally called Soviet assertions that there were only two Chernobyl deaths 'frankly preposterous'.

But by 22 May, more moderate Soviet figures were

grudgingly accepted. The UPI news agency issued a retraction, saying they could no longer support their original claim of 2,000 deaths.

The US nuclear industry, none the less, remained doggedly defensive. President Reagan's closest adviser, chief of staff Donald Regan, set the tone for the American nuclear industry's response to Chernobyl. As the President took a day off on 30 April in Bali on his way to the Tokyo summit, Regan told reporters, 'Nuclear power is a good thing for the future of many nations, including our own – we shouldn't just throw out the baby with the bath water and condemn all nuclear power plants because of this.' Larry Speakes, the White House press aide, added, 'Chernobyl could not happen in the United States because we have a number of facilities to prevent it.'

The opportunity Chernobyl presented to blame the shortcomings of Russian nuclear technologists was quickly taken up in an outburst of chauvinistic pride. It could never happen in America, echoed the nuclear industry leaders; all American reactors have containment structures, they said. None of the Soviet reactors has such a structure, they said. In case the point had been missed, the Atomic Industrial Forum, the American nuclear industry trade association, mailed a letter to reporters which repeated the assertion that the Chernobyl reactor had no containment building. 'The building housing the reactor apparently was constructed for structural rather than containment integrity,' said the letter. A second group, the US Committee for Energy Awareness, which is supported by the electric utilities, declared that 'Many Soviet reactors – including those at Chernobyl – lack such containment structures' (as American reactors have). 'We have not and we will not have a Chernobyl-type plant accident here,' said the industry research arm, the Edison Electrical Institute.

Such displays of extraordinary confidence in the product

have been commonplace throughout the history of the self-assured nuclear business, but it was unusual, to say the least, to find that confidence still brimming over in the wake of Chernobyl. After Three Mile Island, an accident of much lesser degree, the American nuclear industry was downbeat, cautiously forecasting that their plans had been put back from one to three years. They saw orders dropping off – which happened – and calls for improved safety regulations, which also happened. (Indeed, there have been no new orders for nuclear power plants in America since 1978.)

There was no such caution this time. 'Our reactors are pretty safe,' said Carl Walske, the President of the Atomic Industrial Forum, 'we see nothing coming out of this accident to revise that estimate.'

The period of self-congratulation was soon over, however. It rapidly became clear that the Chernobyl accident was relevant to American nuclear reactors, that there were some US reactors of similar, but not identical design; that some US reactors did not have containment structures; that some of the Soviet reactors, including Chernobyl, did; that evacuation plans at US nuclear plants needed overhauling; and that the US reactor safety record had been giving the US government cause for concern.

Finally, the Reagan administration was discovered telling its federal employees to try and avoid talking to the press about Chernobyl – in particular to 'avoid making comparisons' between American reactors and Russian ones. The staff of two government nuclear laboratories were barred from giving out information on nuclear power studies – even those unrelated to the accident. Nuclear critics were quick to point out that 1985 was a particularly bad one for the industry's safety record. As to the administration and industry claim that none of the Soviet plants has a containment structure, this was completely wrong

Several days later a correction was provided by a member of the Nuclear Regulatory Commission (NRC), James Asseltine, who told a congressional committee, 'You cannot just automatically dismiss this accident simply because of a difference in design.' Asseltine revealed that the Soviet reactor at Chernobyl had, in fact, been enclosed in a special safety structure. The NRC had reviewed plans of Chernobyl, which had been lying around untranslated at the the CIA and elsewhere in government agencies, and had concluded that the plant had not one, but two layers of containment, one steel and one concrete. One could withstand pressures of up to 27 lb. per sq. in., the other 57. Most American containments, some of which are of steel and others of reinforced concrete, are built to withstand between 45 and 60 lb., and at least two plants have containments with only 12 and 15 lb. The revelation caused hardly a ripple, however. The American press was more interested in the latest Soviet bulletin – an admission that confusion among local officials had contributed to a 36-hour delay in evacuating people living near the Chernobyl plant. Twelve days later, the *New York Times* resurrected Asseltine's disclosures and ran a front-page story. Chernobyl 'had more safety features than western experts had assumed in the days soon after the accident,' the story began, '[it raised] questions among some experts about the effectiveness of nuclear plant designs in this country.' One member of the NRC admitted, 'Most of the walls around the reactor are truly massive and sturdy.'

The original list of false claims by the government and industry continued. Also wrong was the assertion that all American reactors have containments. In fact, five reactors, run by the Department of Energy for producing plutonium and tritium for nuclear weapons, have no regular containment domes. One of these plants, at Hanford in Washington State, is a graphite-moderated reactor similar to the Chernobyl design. The others are at the Savannah River plant in South Carolina.

US officials claim that these reactors do have different safety structures, principally a 'confinement' building to filter out radioactive particles should they escape from the nuclear core, plus a separate emergency cooling system. Critics contend, however, that if the emergency system failed and a graphite fire plus a hydrogen explosion ensued it would be likely to blow out the confinement, much as at Chernobyl. Moreover, the Hanford reactor, now 22 years old, has been showing signs of age recently. Since January the reactor has been shut down six times because of fuel failures. Also high-level radioactive wastes stored nearby have leaked into the Columbia river causing abnormal levels of radiation.

In fact, the problem of where to store increasing amounts of radioactive wastes was still unresolved in America. Federal officials were looking for new sites but state officials kept turning them down. Chernobyl certainly has not helped the search for a suitable site.

The Soviet accident's greatest potential immediate impact was on the American government's evacuation procedures. Critics said the procedures were in a shambles. (An oft-repeated, true story is that when an emergency plan for the Seabrook, New Hampshire nuclear power plant was tested last February, the emergency telephone distributed to residents was actually the number of the loan department of a local bank.) But, the real concern is that federal regulations only prepare for evacuation of people within a 16-km (10-mile) radius of the plant. 'How do you justify a 16-km (10-mile) evacuation when the Russians, with little regard for public safety, evacuated to 30 km (19 miles),' asked Tom Cochran, a nuclear physicist with the Natural Resources Defense Council, a research and lobbying group.

If these new concerns troubled the American nuclear industry, it did not show. At the end of the third week after the accident, the Atomic Industrial Forum was as aloof as ever. They conceded 'a little simplication' in their original claims. For a more realistic approach to the whole affair, one had to go to Wall Street, where hard-nosed investors saw the potential for another rough ride ahead for the US nuclear industry. Stocks of US electric utility companies fell sharply on 30 April, and contributed to the biggest one-day loss – of about 42 points – in the history of the Dow Jones industrial index.

These reactions around the world took place as, at Chernobyl itself, the struggle with a monster out of control began to assume proportions of life or death.

8 Struggling with a monster

'Nobody in the world before has ever been confronted with an accident of this kind.'
Yevgeny Velikhov, chief scientist at the disaster-site

At Chernobyl, by 4 a.m., just over 2½ hours after the explosion which had destroyed reactor No. 4, frantic phone calls from the plant brought the militia to take charge of the town. One of the first on the scene in the choking darkness was Major-General Gennadi Berdov, a senior militia (police) officer and a deputy minister in the Ukraine Interior Ministry.

Although it was still the middle of the night, there was little time to waste. Under Berdov's command the militia units started blocking all the roads leading in and out of Pripyat, as well as the road to the station, which would soon be used by weekend ramblers on their way to the woods. Every corner and every junction was manned, and staff began drawing up lists and assigning staff to different sectors of the town. Buses were ordered – 1,100 of them – to take part in a massive evacuation of Pripyat's 20,000 inhabitants and another 26,000 in the surrounding countryside, within a radius of 10 km (6 miles). At this stage there were no proposals to evacuate the bigger town of Chernobyl, and another official arriving in Pripyat on Saturday morning was surprised to see wedding parties still in progress.

There was later to be confusion about the timing of the evacuation, with some officials saying that it took place on 27 April, 36 hours after the accident, while others insisted that it took place the same day. The definitive version was given by Boris Semenov in a statement to the board of the IAEA on 21 May. He said: 'Mass evacuation was carried out on 27 April, women and children being evacuated first.' 27 April was also the date given by Morris Rosen, Director of Safety at the IAEA, in a Moscow press conference on 9 May. What in fact seems to have happened is that about 1,000 families living in the immediate plant workers' settlement 1.6 km (1 mile) from the power station were evacuated on Saturday afternoon, 12 hours after the accident, using local transport. To avoid an area of heavy contamination, the plant workers were made to leave by a military pontoon bridge hurriedly thrown across the Pripyat river. But the time taken must have exposed some of these people to high radiation. There was then a crucial bureaucratic confusion. As *Izvestiya* was later to admit, the nuclear plant health authorities controlled only a 2.5 km zone. They had absolutely no contact with the ordinary regional health authorities who administered Pripyat.

The rest of the Pripyat population were taken out the next day, in the 'mass evacuation' referred to by Semenov. Before it could start, Berdov faced a problem. As soon as they heard they were to be moved, people became alarmed. A delegation assembled and came to the Regional Council building to protest. Berdov was deputed to meet them, and fearing strong resistance decided to put on his general's cap, tunic and striped trousers, glittering with gold braid and medal ribbon bars. It worked. 'Someone spoke indignantly,' he said, 'but was quickly shouted down when they understood the danger.'

While the grey-haired Berdov was confronting the delegation, Komsomol (Young Communist League) members were going round the housing blocks, listing everyone living there and telling them what to do. There was to be minimal luggage, and, to prevent panic traffic jams, no use of private cars. According to Berdov's diary, the first column of buses entered the town 'sharp at 2 p.m.'. Few people thought, as they waited to be picked up in front of their homes, that they were leaving for any length of time. The militia were ordered to check every flat to make sure that everyone had left. By 4.20 on Sunday afternoon, according to Boris Shcherbina, head of the Soviet inquiry commission, everybody had been taken out of the town. The victims of radiation, almost all the firemen and plant workers, 18 with severe radiation burns and another 186 with slight or medium radiation injuries, had been taken to hospitals in Moscow and Kiev.

In the departing buses were the wives and families of perhaps 150 workers who had stayed on at the plant to run down the other three reactors and keep safety systems going. In smoke and radiation they had been there since early morning (and in some cases all night), monitoring and manning the cooling circuits. Knowing full well the risks they were running, they had taken it in shifts, because without their presence any one of the other reactors could have gone the same way as No. 4.

The reactor most at risk was No. 3. It shared the same chimney as No. 4 and its block was part of the same building complex, separated by a none-too-thick series of walls from the burning mass next door.

The engineer Vladimir Lyamets had been working only 200 yards from No. 4 reactor when the explosion took place, but had refused to leave his post. He stayed there more than 48 hours, and agreed to enter hospital only on 30 April 'when he found it hard to go on fighting the ailment' – radiation sickness. Another technician, Arkadi Uskov, had been in the adjoining No. 3 block when he realized that something serious had happened. He had run to his boss, Vladimir Chagunov. Together they had tried to reach No. 4, but had found everything dark, because of an electricity failure, and the way blocked by debris. Uskov says he knew that he had to keep his own reactor cooling system going, and wanted to set up an alternative water flow. He went to get help from the turbine controller, Andrei Turmodin, but by now the fire was threatening the turbine room, and they had to struggle just to prevent its spread.

Radiation technician Nikolai Gorbachenko was in block No. 4 keeping a second-by-second check on radiation readings. When he saw a sudden increase in the dose rate, he started leading people out. Time and again he went back into the darkened, smoke-filled irradiated building, even though, because of his job, he knew the score. He remained the last in his section, and when he finally came out, refused to be taken to a safe place.

Numerous other cases were later to come to light of workers who had refused to leave their places, even when ordered to do so by medical staff or the police. In some cases courage may have stemmed from ignorance of the full extent of the danger. But all the evidence is that, even when they were made aware of it, it made no difference. Now and later, whether simply sticking at their jobs, or seeking to tame the monster by dousing it with sand or burrowing underneath, the 'fighters' of Chernobyl showed the same reckless, suicidal courage that their predecessors had done in the fight against Hitler over these same Ukrainian marshes in 1941.

But, as in 1941, there was another side to the picture. 'You cannot hide a sin,' declared the Kiev Regional Communist Party leader, Grigori Revenko, talking to the newspaper *Sovietskaya Rossiya* on 7 May. 'Individual workers were found who in difficult conditions did not display the necessary will and steadfastness to be in the front line.'

'There were those who cracked under the pressure,' said another Party worker – and not just among employees at the plant. A week after the first emergencies Party officials found it necessary to expel a 30-year-old member, V. Malofienko, who, pretending to be sick, had deserted his post as head of a team decontaminating the evacuation buses. Two members had to be expelled from the Pripyat Komsomol – a construction worker, Yuri Zagalski, for 'giving priority to his own welfare', and a girl section secretary, Galina Luppiye, for running away to her parents.

A committee of the Pripyat Party had also to discipline three of its members for dereliction of duty towards evacuees from their transport unit. According to *Pravda*, in ten days A. Sicharenko and A. Shapoval did nothing to help their subordinates. They failed to pay their wages on time, gave people no clothing, and ignored legitimate calls for help. Shapoval was expelled and Sicharenko given a reprimand (a severe blow to his career), as was also the unit's Party secretary, A. Gubsky, for 'failure to assess the situation'.

That there were other cases of dereliction and cowardice, mainly among ancillary workers, might be fairly deduced from *Pravda*'s admission that in the 'tight corners revealed by the accident, some officials turned out to be psycologically unready' and by Revenko's blunt use in another interview of the word 'desertions'.

Outside Pripyat, in the farms and villages where radiation levels were high, some of the peasants were reluctant to leave. 'A few old women took some persuading,' one of those responsible for the evacuation told *Izvestia*.

They even hid in the cellars. You would find them there and they would say: 'My dear! Just look how the orchard is blossoming! Who will look after it? Who is going to feed all the chickens and the ducks? They would never forgive me.' Inevitably there were tears, and one man was seen embracing his dog, saying goodbye to it as if it were human.

The evacuation convoys stretched for nearly 20 km, and even Soviet war veterans could not remember such a mass resettlement of people in such a short time. There were, inevitably, hitches, mainly in providing clothing and footwear, and some of those responsible were anxious about what kind of response the evacuees would get when they arrived to be billeted at very short notice on families unprepared for their arrival. In fact the evacuees seem to have been made welcome everywhere, and the canteen at one collective farm, which had prepared lunch for the new arrivals, found it had no customers. The families where the evacuees had been billeted insisted on feeding them themselves.

Even while the fleet of buses was delivering the 46,000 evacuees from Pripyat and other settlements to their reception areas north of Kiev, another fleet – this time of helicopters – was arriving near Chernobyl from the stations of the Soviet Air Force in western Russia and the Ukraine.

It was preceded to Chernobyl by Air Force Major-General Nikolai Antoshkin, who had been reached by telephone on Saturday evening after scientists had assessed the damage at the power station and told Moscow the terrible truth – that the plant had a graphite fire and that a plume of radioactive particles 3,000 feet (914 metres) high was shooting upwards from the burning reactor.

A video taken of the crippled reactor at this time, and later shown to western experts, provided vivid evidence of the appalling problems the Russians faced. It showed the destruction of the core and the graphite burning, a quarter of it glowing red hot. 'It was grilling like a charcoal fire,' one witness said. The temperature of the fire was around 2,500 °C, which was pushing radioactivity high up into the atmosphere in a 'chimney' effect.

Just whose idea it was to use helicopters to try to seal the fire is not clear. It could have come from the military or from the team of scientists there being hastily gathered round the energetic Vice-President of the Soviet Academy of Sciences, Yevgeny Velikhov. But one thing stands out.

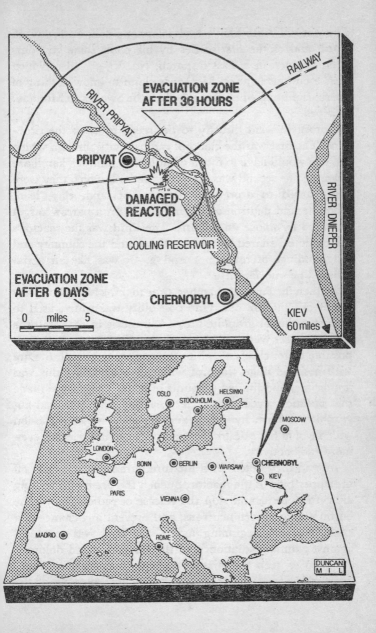

The date of Antoshkin's first telephone call, Saturday 26 April, and of the first sorties by his pilots some 36 hours later, is given in a Tass dispatch, No. V5-38, all of which casts a curious light on Moscow's claim to know nothing of a serious mishap when first asked by the Swedes on Monday, 28 April.

Antoshkin went directly to the scene to assess the problems. The first was the cloud of radioactivity through which his men would have to fly on what looked almost a kamikaze mission. The second was the precision with which they were being asked to drop their 'bombs' of sand, clay, lead, dolomite and neutron-absorbing boron on a narrow target obscured by smoke and debris. The third was the reactor's tall chimney, shared by reactor No. 3, and the chimney and tall buildings of reactors 1 and 2. 'It was like an aerial slalom,' he said later.

By then the Russians had had time to think about how they might put the fire out. One possibility was water, used to quench a similar graphite fire at Windscale in 1957, but the circumstances were not identical. At Windscale it had been possible to get close enough to the reactor to quench the fire with a single huge wave of water; at Chernobyl this was impossible, and limited amounts of water might have made the situation even worse, by reacting with the red-hot graphite to form hydrogen and set off a major explosion which would have destroyed reactor No. 3 and released even more radioactivity.

Instead they opted for a mixture of materials to close off the upper part of the reactor, quench the fire by preventing air getting to it, and stop the release of radioactivity. The boron was to absorb neutrons, and prevent any chance of a chain reaction beginning again, the lead was to shield against gamma radiation, and the sand, clay and dolomite designed to keep the mixture together and make it homogeneous, as well as absorbing as much as possible of the fission products. It was a technique that had never been tried before, but it worked. 'They had a unique situation, unparalleled, and they dealt with it very well,' says one western expert.

The plan adopted was to position a ground controller with a clear optical (and probably also radar) view of both the damaged reactor and the helicopter's approach path. With the help of the electronic counterparts of a stop-watch and compass, the controller would signal the crews as to the precise moment to release their loads of materials. In addition, a monitoring plane flew alongside, providing further information to help in accurate dropping. The first flights were the most difficult, as the crater in the top of the reactor made a small target and the radiation levels were dangerously high, which meant that the pilots had to fly in and out in a matter of seconds. For the first flights they carried a single sack, pushed out of the cargo door by hand. But technicians soon designed a quick-release device that enabled the pilots to drop six to eight sacks at a time, slung from a net below the machine.

On the first day the pilots – some sporting the moustaches fashionable among veterans of Afghanistan – flew 93 sorties, on the second 186. To begin with none knew how much radiation they were receiving and there were reports among Soviet journalists that a number had suffered serious radiation injuries, and were evacuated for treatment in military hospitals. On later flights, temporary lead aprons and shields were improvised to limit the dose.

By the time the last opening had been sealed and the whole reactor covered with its 'dome' of neutron-absorbing materials, the helicopters had dropped some 5,000 tonnes. When the missions ended on 13 May, Semenov told a press conference in Vienna, the reactor had 'to all intents and purposes stopped releasing fission products into the atmosphere' – the successful struggle had taken at least 14 days and had needed a large fleet of helicopters and pilots. Nevertheless, Yevgeny Velikhov, the Kremlin's chief scientific troubleshooter, still looked unshaven and haggard when he appeared among the crowds in the stifling underground bunker used as the plant's emergency command post. One threat was over. But he knew that another potential catastrophe was looming.

Velikhov was a compact energetic figure with, in normal times, a ready smile. He is a close personal friend both of the Soviet leader Mikhail Gorbachev and his wife Raisa. Gorbachev had met the scientist, three years younger than him, when they were both at university, and they had risen together in Soviet society. Velikhov had been working on magnetic plasmas at the Troitsk high-energy laser centre before the disaster dispatched him on the first plane to the Ukraine: he is believed by US officials to head Gorbachev's 'Star Wars' programme in answer to that of President Reagan's. He also heads the team from the Academy of Sciences that has been talking with an unofficial team of US counterparts about test-ban verification.

The only reason that he remains merely deputy head of the Academy appears to be that Gorbachev does not wish him to waste his valuable time on ceremony and protocol: very top talent like Velikhov's is in short supply in the Soviet Union. He was now facing his hardest challenge: on Velikhov's scientific skills rested not only the reputation of the Soviet Union in the eyes of the world, but the fate of perhaps hundreds of thousands of its citizens.

The flow of poisons from the reactor had been staunched, and the fire quenched, but not without running a serious risk. The mass of material on top of the reactor presented two dangers: that it would insulate it so effectively that radioactive decay heat would raise its temperature to a meltdown, or that the structure of the reactor, weakened by the intense fire, would collapse under the weight. In the first case, the Russians would be fighting a 'China Syndrome'; in the second, the danger of an explosion as the hot materials from the reactor core came into contact with water lying in a pool beneath the core, designed to catch water released in a loss-of-coolant accident.

It was vital for the Russian team to preserve the damaged core as best they could, and hope that it would support the mass of material now lying on top of it. For this reason, they decided not to use liquid nitrogen as a coolant inside the reactor building, for fear the intense cold would crack the supports and send the core crashing down. They did use ordinary nitrogen as an inert gas to bathe the core, an insurance against further fires. Liquid nitrogen was later used to freeze the soil beneath the reactor.

As it happened there was no 'China Syndrome'. The reactor at Chernobyl may have had some design faults, but the chances of a full fuel meltdown were certainly less than they would have been for a pressurized-water reactor in a similarly crippled condition. This is because the fuel in the Chernobyl reactor is contained in many different channels, separated by graphite blocks, while in a PWR it is all inside the same pressure vessel and can accumulate in a large molten pool at the bottom. The graphite that survived the fire meant that the meltdown of fuel was much more localized than it would have been in a light-water reactor.

At the time, however, the Russians did not realize this, and behind the bland front being presented to the world there was a real terror that the fuel would melt through the floor, reaching the water table and polluting drinking water for miles around. The first problem – and it was desperately urgent – was to get rid of the tens of thousands of gallons of water in the cavity below the reactor. If the molten mass of graphite and uranium sank into it, the hydrogen generated would cause an explosion many times more deadly than the first.

To drain this and, further, to lower the immediately surrounding water table, literally hundreds of fire engines were summoned from the whole Kiev region. (Ten days later, 92 were still standing near the reactor site, contaminated and not yet able to be moved.) But there was still water left in the lowest pool beneath the core. To get rid of it, it was necessary to open two valves which now lay deep under radioactive water, and which could be reached only through narrow passages, flooded and completely dark.

Two engineers, Alexei Ananenko (who knew where the valves were) and Valeri Bezpalov, volunteered to go down below the reactor, with a third man, Boris Baranov, holding a lamp. Wearing diving suits, the three made their way through a series of flooded passages and finally reached the valves by feeling along a pipe, after the lamp had failed. Ananenko said to *Sovietskaya Rossiya*:

> We tried to turn it – it moved. Our hearts pounded with joy, but we couldn't say anything – we were wearing respirators. I showed Valeri the other valve. It budged too. A few minutes later the characteristic noise or splashing sound was heard – the water was gone. A few minutes after that they were hugging us.

The next immediate need was to thicken the concrete platform beneath the reactor to begin the job of encasing it in a concrete 'sarcophagus'. The only way was to drive a tunnel under the beast, but tunnelling was at first thought impossible in the spongy and part-waterlogged Pripyat soil. A solution was suggested by engineers with experience of building the Leningrad Metro, also on such soil. It was to drill holes at a relatively flat angle to freeze the soil, using liquid nitrogen, so that the tunnel-cutting machine blades could get a bite on it. It was tried and worked.

Operating at ground level, excavating machines with

protective lead sheets over the control cabs prepared the ground for drilling and pumping in nitrogen; the soil was frozen, and tunnelling began. First, they dug a trench, to install the tunnelling machines, and began drilling from close to No. 3 reactor towards No. 4. Within a week 400 men working in three-hour shifts in protective clothing had built a tunnel 135 metres (450 feet) long and were 5.4 metres (18 feet) below the reactor. The cement works at Vyshgorod near Kiev had been ordered to produce as much cement as possible, and in ten days had equalled their normal two-month output. From the works the concrete was shipped to the edge of the 30-km zone around the crippled reactor, and carried the rest of the way in dump trucks.

The task was to build a bed, or 'cushion' underneath the reactor. Inside the concrete, the technicians planned to install cooling circuits to take away any heat that found its way down from the core. The bed will form the base of a concrete structure which will enclose the whole reactor, entombing it for the hundreds or thousands of years which will be needed before its radioactivity has fallen to a safe level. In effect, the Russian teams have been forced to design, engineer and build a radioactive waste dump, above ground, and in conditions of high radiation. It is a task that has never been attempted before.

The other urgent job was to prevent the radioactivity scattered around the power station site from escaping into the Pripyat river. Here the Russians were lucky, for no rain fell in the days immediately after the disaster, and radioactive dust that had settled had no opportunity to be washed into the river. On 4 May, workers with teams of bulldozers began the construction of 7.5 km of dykes along the banks of the Pripyat, and around the whole power station site, using soil and peat. The job was given, in what must have seemed the dream of a sadistic sergeant-major, to an army battalion just back from Afghanistan. Other battalions of soldiers were conscripts –

called-up into the reserves from their spring-time work in the fields all over the Ukraine.

If rain had fallen before the job was finished, it would have been 'very complex', the Ukrainian Premier, Alexander Lyashko, admitted. Three hundred deep wells in the city of Kiev were ready to be connected to the mains as an emergency supply of drinking water and another 100 were being dug.

But by the time the rain fell in earnest around 20 May, the dykes were complete and covered in polythene sheeting. Intercepting trenches had also been dug, to catch the rainfall before it reached the dykes. According to the engineers responsible, the makeshift system worked, and prevented any rainfall reaching the Pripyat river. The earth in the dykes, particularly those around the power station itself, included some chemicals designed to absorb any radioactive materials reaching them.

By 11 May, Velikhov was able to declare that a turning point had been reached. 'Until now,' he declared, 'the possibility of a catastrophe really did exist: a great quantity of fuel and graphite of the reactor was in an incandescent state. Now this is not the case.' (No mention of this potential catastrophe had been made by any Soviet leader until it had been averted.) Now, he said, a new stage of the work was beginning – decontaminating the power station and its surroundings, and isolating it as completely as possible from the environment. But while for the engineers there might be time to slacken the hectic pace, an army of doctors, officials and Party workers was struggling to cope with the problems of the evacuees. The initial evacuation of Pripyat had been conducted in a relatively orderly fashion (though as we have seen, rather late) and in obedience to an instruction in the voluminous handbook relating to the RBMK reactor that 'in case of emergency, panic can sometimes be more dangerous than radiation'.

Even so, evidence was soon to emerge that the time taken to get people out had been dangerously long. Among the radiation sufferers interviewed later in hospital was a young woman Komsomol worker, Anyeliye Petrovskaya, who had been rounding up families and helping them on to buses. The disclosure three weeks later that some 1,000 people had been checked for acute radiation injury, including some from the settlement of Pripyat, is a further indication that there was at least a day's indecision after the accident. Near the end of the first week the lack of direction from Kiev, masked by bland pronouncements about 'liquidating the consequences of the accident', appears to have affected the front-line too. Most serious of all was the failure of the Ukrainian authorities to carry out the evacuation of a much wider area, including the city of Chernobyl, which had now been subjected to a steady fall-out of radioactive particles for seven days.

Moscow's intervention was a turning point. Hearing for the first time from Premier Nikolai Ryzhkov and Central Committee Secretary Yegor Ligachov the extent of the Ukrainian cover-up, Mikhail Gorbachev was reportedly in a high state of anger. Heads rolled (it may never be known how many, but in the end they will almost certainly turn out to include that of the Ukrainian Party chief, Vladimir Shcherbitsky); orders were immediately given to evacuate a much wider 30-km (19-mile) zone; and the entire best brains of the Soviet Union were assembled to tackle the problems.

At last the evacuation of Chernobyl and the surrounding area went ahead, nine days after the accident. This second evacuation involved 30,000 people from Chernobyl, as well as the inhabitants of numerous collective farms, together with tens of thousands of cattle and other farm animals. The principle adopted was to take each farm as a whole to its 'host' farm. As in the earlier evacuation, the reception area was some 96–112 km (60–70 miles) to the south, in the countryside north of Kiev.

By 6 May the announced total, evidently involving a recount, was 92,000. They were being attended by 1,300 doctors and dosimetrists, with a fleet of 240 ambulances to take those found to be irradiated to hospital. Most of those interviewed by journalists, including a four-man 'pool' of the western press, appeared in good heart. But by the end of the month, Party workers were beginning to wonder how to deal with things if the situation were greatly prolonged.

All evacuees were given an immediate cash grant of 200 roubles (nearly £200) by the State; village shops were ordered to give credit for food and clothing; school-places were found and, officials said, work. But the disruption to everyday life and in many cases family ties must have been traumatic. Most had left home with only a handful of belongings (and what they had left behind was contaminated); many in their haste had had to leave pets; and as expulsions and reprimands showed, in some cases Party officials had neglected their people's welfare. One of the problems was finding sufficient food for the vast herds of cattle. Nine collective farms in one area had suddenly to find the feed for an extra 17,446 cows, which had to be milked as well. 'They are racking their brains wondering how to find sufficient food,' one official admitted. Nearby farms were ordered to provide extra straw and silage to keep the cows alive.

In the 30-km (19-mile) zone around Chernobyl and Pripyat, the only people moving around were in the trucks bringing supplies to the stricken reactor, and the militia patrolling the deserted streets. The streets were eerily clean and fresh. They were continuously being hosed down. From time to time people managed to slip back through the cordons to their houses, only to be detected by the militia and removed again. 'It's quiet and calm, it's eerie,' one

militia man said. As time passes, it will become more difficult to prevent people from returning to the homes they left
in such haste, but the possibility of being permitted to return
home soon does not seem high. Will people be allowed to go
back to Pripyat? 'Well of course, being sensible, I hardly
think so, in the near future,' Velikhov said on 26 May. 'I do
not see any particular sense in a rapid return to the settlement.'

The date of any return will depend on how successful the
Russians are in tackling another unique problem – the
decontamination of buildings, fields, streets and homes
covered with dangerous amounts of radioactive dust. Regular bulletins from the authorities have insisted that radiation
levels are falling, and there is no reason to doubt this. Since
much of the pollution was caused by iodine-131, its relatively rapid decay would ensure falling levels of radiation
even if the Russians were to do nothing around Chernobyl.
But the decline in iodine-131 will not be enough, because
other much longer-lived isotopes were also released, and
these must also be mopped up. The problem is being tackled
in a number of ways, some of them novel, others familiar
from the experience of nuclear weapons testing.

The first task was to prevent the spread of the radioactive
dust out of the region around the crippled reactor. The
dykes to protect the Pripyat river were a first priority, but
the Russians also adopted a simple method of preventing
material being carried out of the 30-km (19-mile) zone on
vehicles. They erected a 'ring-fence' (it is not clear whether
this is literally a fence, or simply a circle on the map) and
blocked all access by road or rail to the area inside. All
'clean' vehicles carrying materials stopped at the line before
transferring their loads to a shuttle system of contaminated
trucks which went to and fro between the line and the
reactor. In general, railway wagons were preferred to trucks,
because it is easier to clean contamination off steel wheels

than off rubber tyres. Transport within the danger-zone close to the plant was by armoured car: the military drivers, squinting at dosimeters by their feet, learned rapidly to avoid the 'pockets' of radioactive debris that littered the ground.

Scrupulous attention has also had to be paid to the clothing worn by those close to the reactor – most of it has had to be thrown away after a single day's wear. Even the dazzling military uniform General Berdov put on to persuade the reluctant citizens of Pripyat to join the evacuation had to join other more humble garments in bins for collecting low-level waste. The only item he saved was the insignia of Meritorious Worker of the USSR Ministry of Internal Affairs. He unclipped that, and reluctantly threw the rest away.

Some initial estimates about the decontamination were absurdly optimistic. *Izvestia* reported one official as saying that the outer surfaces of the buildings, starting with the roofs, would be washed, the waste water being directed down special channels into tanks constructed for the purpose. The topsoil would be removed in the danger zone, and the whole area concreted over. 'When this work is finished the Chernobyl power station will be operational again,' he declared.

In fact, the problems were a good deal worse than that. First, the reactor building had to be isolated to prevent any further leakages of radioactive materials. Welders were sent in to seal doors, and strip down the electricity circuits. They were told exactly what to do, and given just 12 minutes to do it, since in that time they accumulated a full dose of radiation. Then they were checked for radioactivity and – if the dose was low enough – sent in again. Seventy tonnes of lead shot, dropped by helicopter, was used to seal some openings.

The effluent drainage system to the Pripyat river had to

be sealed off, and alternative tanks provided to catch rainfall draining from the building. Five steel tanks were ordered and built at high speed. To reduce the amounts of radioactive dust carried off the roofs by rain, a variety of methods were tried. 'Water glass' – potassium or sodium silicate solutions – was spread on roofs to seal in the dust. On other surfaces where substantial chunks of rubble or debris were left after the explosions, a form of liquid synthetic rubber was applied by helicopter. On contact with air it quickly hardened, covering the polluted areas with film, described by one official as a white 'quilt', designed to seal in the radioactivity.

For other areas, where dust rather than rubble was the problem, an alternative was tried. The ground was sprayed with a plastic film, which hardens to form a material very much like polyethylene sacking. On cooling and drying, it is supposed to grip the dust and other small litter so tightly that the film formed can be rolled up like a carpet and disposed of. In some areas, radioactive rubble has been bulldozed away, using radio-controlled earthmoving equipment or specially designed infra-red robots. Some were shipped in from West Germany: others designed and rigged up by Soviet engineers. They had to operate in high heat and radioactivity. The material collected has all been dumped in the large hole dug originally to form the foundations of the No. 5 reactor. This conveniently-placed pit will now form a buried waste dump on the power station site, and another location will have to be found for the No. 5 reactor, if it is ever to be built.

The farmland and forests around the power station presented other difficulties. Valeri Brezhnev, the Deputy Minister of Forest Industry, admitted on Moscow radio on 25 May that it would undoubtedly be necessary to fell the plantations of young coniferous trees in some areas and bury them. In other places trees would have to be felled to provide what he called 'building approach lines and various industrial construction sites', presumably for the continuing task of stabilizing the reactor. One of the greatest dangers was forest fires, which would release the radioactivity which had settled on the trees and send it back into the atmosphere. Helicopters with parachutists are patrolling the forests, and will be dropped to extinguish forest fires should any start. On farmland, the process of trying to find a solution began only on 20 May, with some experimental ploughing of affected land to see how deeply the radioactivity had penetrated. Officials have talked of planting species which will accumulate the radioactivity from the soil, although presumably they could not then be used for food.

The workers involved in all these tasks have been accumulating substantial doses of radioactivity. Each has carried a personal dosimeter to provide an estimate of the dose. 'How much have you caught?' one welder asked another as they consulted their dosimeters at the end of a shift assembling pipes. The answer was not recorded, but another worker did reveal that those close to the plant were getting a year's dose – 10 rems – in a fortnight. (The figure of 10 rems, double the annual limit for radiation workers, is the level appropriate in 'emergency conditions', Soviet officials claim.) Some reactor-site workers were being allowed 25 rems.

As the task of stabilizing the reactor and cleaning up the mess proceeded, Soviet officials who had been initially silent became more forthcoming and more frank. On 3 May, Tass had denied that this was the greatest nuclear disaster in history, but by the end of May Soviet officals at all levels were conceding that it was. Valentin Falin, head of the Novosti Press Agency, admitted in an interview in *Der Spiegel* on 11 May that those at the power station had 'in part failed' in their jobs, particularly because the 'content and quantity of information communicated to Moscow was neither sufficient nor correct'. In the Soviet Union, he said, 'We were not prepared for such an accident, we had not basically foreseen any instructions in advance,' and much took place 'without coherence'.

This certainly seems to be true. The first clear details of the accident were given to the west by Boris Yeltsin, in an interview on West German TV on 2 May, but in the Soviet Union this information had still not been conveyed to the people by 7 May. There have been persistent attempts to pretend that the first evacuation from Pripyat took place a day sooner than it did, and Soviet spokesmen have consistently – if understandably – sought to miminize the significance of the accident. Much of their energies has been spent in denouncing the western media for exaggeration and misreporting. In this they have some justification, though prompt supplies of reliable and credible information would have prevented the worst excesses. The most celebrated of these was the claim by the press agency United Press International, based on a call from a resident of Kiev, that 2,000 had died in the disaster. Other western media exaggerations were too absurd to be seen as malevolent. The *New York Post* ran a headline declaring that 15,000 people killed by the accident had been bulldozed into a mass grave – but nobody seeks serious news from the *New York Post*. And Italian TV ran pictures of a plant which it said was the smouldering wreck of the Chernobyl power station, still pouring smoke. In fact, they had been hoaxed – it was a peaceful cement works near Trieste. One of the American networks, ABC, overexcited by this great scoop, ran the pictures without checking, and 24 hours later had to make a shamefaced apology.

When General Secretary Mikhail Gorbachev finally appeared on Soviet TV on 14 May, he did convey more information and made no attempt to pretend that the accident had not been a desperately serious one. But to western viewers, and perhaps to some Soviet ones, the broadcast seemed strangely short of the 'openness' which he had promised would be a feature of his style of leadership. So it was, but it must be understood in the light of his resolve to be sure of the facts before saying or doing anything that might damage confidence in his plans for managerial and economic reform. The human errors behind the tragedy at Chernobyl seemed to epitomize all those failures in management that he had pledged himself to uproot. It might strengthen his hand in future – but in another sense he had arrived in power too late.

Gorbachev's broadcast was none the less unprecedented. He began sombrely:

Good evening, comrades! You all know – a misfortune has recently befallen us – the accident at Chernobyl nuclear power station. It has sorely affected Soviet people and perturbed the international public. For the first time we actually came face-to-face with such terrible power as is presented by nuclear energy out of control. . . . A commission was formed, which immediately went out to the site of the incident and, in the Politburo, a group was set up under the leadership of Nikolay Ivanovich Ryzhkov to examine operational matters.

All the work is essentially being conducted round the clock. The whole country's scientific, technical and economic potential has been put into action. . . .

What exactly happened?

As the specialists report, during planned decommissioning of the No. 4 generating set, the power of the reactor suddenly increased. The considerable discharge of steam and subsequent reaction led to the formation of hydrogen, its explosion, the destruction of the reactor and the radioactive emission connected with it.

At present it is still too early to make a definitive judgment on the causes of the accident. . . .

'It was the first time that we had come up against this sort of emergency, where the dangerous power of the out-of-control atom had to be rapidly curbed and the scale of the accident had to be restricted to the utmost.

The seriousness of the situation was obvious. It needed to be urgently and authoritatively evaluated. And as soon as we received reliable initial information, it was made available to Soviet people and was sent through diplomatic channels to the governments of foreign countries. . . .

Inhabitants of the station settlement were evacuated within hours and then, when it became clear that there was a potential threat to the health of people in the adjacent zone, they were also evacuated to safe areas. This entire complicated job required extreme speed, organization and precision. . . .

Thanks to the effective measures that have been adopted, it can be said today that the worst is over. It has proved possible to avert the most serious consequences. Of course, it is too early to draw the final line under the incident. We must not rest content. There is still a great deal of lengthy work ahead. The radiation level in the power station zone and the territory directly adjoining it currently still remains a danger to human health. . . .

In the world as a whole, and this must be stressed, there has been understanding for the calamity which has befallen us and for our action in this difficult situation. We are profoundly grateful to our friends among the socialist countries who have shown solidarity with the Soviet people at a difficult time. We are indebted to the politicians and public figures in other countries for their sincere sympathy and support. We express our goodwill towards the foreign scientists and specialists who showed their readiness to provide assistance to overcome the consequences of the accident. I should like to note the participation of the American doctors . . . in treating the sick, and also to thank the business circles in those countries which responded rapidly to our request to purchase certain types of equipment, materials and medicines. We duly appreciate the objective attitude to events at Chernobyl nuclear power station adopted by the International Atomic Energy Agency and its Director-General, Hans Blix. In other words, we highly appreciate the sympathy of all those people who have responded with open hearts to our misfortune and our problems.

However, one cannot overlook the political assessment made and the reaction to the event in Chernobyl by the governments, politicians and mass media in certain NATO countries, particularly the USA. They unleashed an unbridled anti-Soviet campaign. What they have lately said and written defies description – the 'thousands of deaths', the 'communal graves of those killed', 'Kiev deserted', the fact that 'the entire land of the Ukraine is contaminated', and so on and so forth. In general we came up against a real heap of lies, the most unscrupulous and malevolent lies. And although it is not pleasant to recall all this, it is necessary. It is necessary so that the international public may be aware of what we were up against. . . .

All they needed was a line they could grasp in order to discredit the Soviet Union and its foreign policy, weaken the impact of the Soviet proposals for ending nuclear tests and eliminate nuclear weapons, and at the same time soften the growing criticism of the USA's behaviour in the international arena and its militaristic course. . . .

We interpreted this tragedy in quite a different manner. We understand: this is yet another ring on the tocsin, yet another stern warning that the nuclear age requires fresh political thinking and fresh policies. . . .

As for the 'insufficiency' of information, around which a special campaign was launched – moreover, one which was political in content and nature – the question in this instance is an invented one. The following confirms that this is so. Everyone remembers that the American authorities needed 10 days to inform their own Congress, and months to let the world community know, what a tragedy had occurred at the Three Mile Island nuclear power station in 1979. I have already said how we acted. . . .

But the essential thing is something else. We consider that the accident at Chernobyl nuclear power station, just like the accidents at American, British and other nuclear power stations, faces all states with very serious questions which require a responsible attitude. Today there are more than 370 nuclear reactors operating in various countries of the world. This is the reality. It is difficult to imagine the future of the world economy without the development of nuclear power. . . .

What might one have in mind here? First, international measures for the safe development of nuclear power engineering should be drawn up on the basis of close co-operation between all states. . . . Within the framework of such measures there must be arranged a system of prompt notification and provision of information in the case of breakdowns and defects. Equally, an international mechanism needs to be arranged with a view to the quickest possible rendering of mutual assistance when dangerous situations arise. . . .

The accident at Chernobyl has once again illustrated just what an abyss would open up if nuclear war should befall mankind. Indeed, the stockpiled nuclear arsenals are fraught with thousands of catastrophes much more terrible than Chernobyl.

As concern about nuclear issues has become more international, the Soviet government, having weighed up all the circumstances connected with the security of its people and all of mankind, has decided to extend its unilateral moratorium on nuclear testing to 6 August this year, that is, to the anniversary of the dropping of the first atomic bomb, which brought death to hundreds of thousands of people, in the Japanese town of Hiroshima more than 40 years ago. . . .

I confirm my proposal to President Reagan, to meet without delay in the capital of any European state that may be prepared to receive us or, say, in Hiroshima, and reach agreement on a ban on nuclear tests.

There was some international disappointment that Gorbachev had veered off into political point-scoring, particularly with what seemed his rather calculated evocation of the memory of Hiroshima.

There was also one area on which Gorbachev had remained mute. Any leader, east or west, would have probably played it down in the same way, for it was the one issue which threatened the whole basis of nuclear energy in the twentieth century. What was really going to be the long-term medical effect of the radiation from Chernobyl on the hundreds of thousands of human beings who were receiving it?

9 A poisoned inheritance

'To hide the real state of affairs is impossible.'
Andrey Vorobyov, Academy of Medical Science,
Moscow, 15 May 1986

Disastrous as it was, the night of 26 April 1986 had its lucky
side for the people of the Ukraine. At first sight, this assertion beggars belief. Many lost relatives and friends to the
fierce radiation from the naked core of the No. 4 reactor.
Thousands more will die of cancers over the next decades,
and many of their children and their children's children may
suffer from genetic diseases. Tens of thousands may not
safely be able to return to their contaminated homes for
years to come. But these appalling consequences could have
been infinitely worse.

If it had not been for some simultaneously lucky factors,
there would have been much more of a holocaust. The accident started at night, so there were only hundreds, not
thousands, on duty at the plant. Even more important, the
people in the towns and countryside around were indoors.
Their homes shielded them from 90 per cent of the immediate radiation. A second factor was the very fierceness of
the graphite fire. Its intense heat sent radioactive materials
high into the air, as if they were contained in an invisible
chimney. This towering column rose more than 1, 200 metres
(4, 000 feet) into the sky. As a result, most radioactivity did
not fall on the surrounding area. Instead, it was widely dispersed on the winds. The longer it stayed in the air, the
more the cloud's short-lived radionuclides decayed, and the
less virulent they became. The weather was responsible for
other pieces of good fortune. The night was still enough to
allow the radioactive plume to rise steadily. What wind there
was blew from the south-east, sending the cloud over the

relatively sparsely-populated Pripet Marshes and forest land. The first, especially deadly discharge just missed Pripyat. Most important of all, for days there was no rain to bring down the radioactive materials.

As one international expert put it: 'If the weather conditions had been wrong, they would have been evacuating people not to settlements, but straight into hospitals.' Leading authorities agree that thousands could easily have died in the first months. This is scarcely surprising. U.S. studies had already predicted the likelihood of thousands of deaths within the first phase of any major nuclear accident. Yet at Chernobyl, there were only 31 'prompt' deaths in the end.

The very factors that mitigated the medical effects of the accident increased its political fall-out throughout the rest of Europe, where the attenuated radioactivity eventually drifted to earth. This did much to fuel the confusion and suspicion that followed the disaster. Western experts, deprived of Soviet data, had to rely on radiation measurements from Sweden. Those levels were so high that, on a conventional basis, they could have meant only one thing — that the people around Chernobyl were suffering from truly enormous exposures and that U.S. predictions were coming true. The experts knew nothing of the factors which had kept the worst fall-out away from the immediate vicinity. As a result, the U.S. administration and the media built up ghoulish scenarios.

Meanwhile, Soviet officials in Moscow were reacting with equal suspicion to western evidence. They too were ignorant of the freak weather conditions which had caused the high radiation readings in Scandinavia. These readings did not tally with local information, and the Russians concluded they were the inventions of a western propaganda campaign. But they were putting out their own misinformation. One official announced the accident would have 'no lasting effect on anyone', a statement that even the vehemently pro-nuclear

Lord Marshall in Britain found 'hard to believe'. On Tuesday 29 April Intourist head office in Moscow said the accident had 'in no way affected the environs even in the proximity of the station', while the Tass news agency curtly admitted to only two deaths, the workers who, as it turned out, had been killed in the chemical explosion itself. The next day, the Kremlin said that 197 people had been taken to hospital, of whom 49 had been quickly discharged. When Mikhail Gorbachev finally broke his silence, 18 days after the accident, he admitted that 299 people were then in hospital.

Eleven thousand miles away, an American doctor leapt at the calamity. At 40, Dr Robert Gale, an associate professor at UCLA, was one of the world's leading authorities on bone-marrow transplants. Slim and soft-spoken, he had built up a reputation for his aggressive pioneering, which cost $100,000 an operation. He had long since laid plans for an emergency as head of the International Bone Marrow Transplant Registry, an organisation that links 128 medical centres in 60 countries. 'A nuclear accident didn't catch us off-guard,' he was to explain. 'This was something we had given considerable thought to.' As soon as he heard of the disaster, he rang Dr Armand Hammer, a colourful 87-year-old oil millionaire. Hammer's friendships with President Reagan and Prince Charles go alongside a fellowship with Soviet leaders stretching back to Lenin. He cabled Gorbachev, saying Gale was ready to help. Within 18 hours, the offer had been accepted.

On 2 May, a jet-lagged Gale arrived with Dr Paul Terasaki of UCLA at the 1,000-bed Municipal Hospital No. 6 on the outskirts of Moscow. They found the 9-story brown brick building 'like a battlefield'. As in the First World War, the casualties were sorted ruthlessly into three groups — those who would die no matter what; those who needed immediate help; and those who might recover without quick attention. Help was given only to the middle group. By this process,

Gale selected 19 out of the 35 most critically ill patients. Many were in a terrible condition. They were badly burned, hairless and racked with infections. Some had begun vomiting with radiation sickness, and others were on the brink of developing spontaneous internal bleeding. Gale and his staff had to take extensive precautions to guard themselves against their patients, including wearing protective clothing and film badges. 'Some tissue we removed was radioactive,' Gale recounted. 'We had blood, urine and stool samples, all radioactive. This is not something we were used to. We all had to be extremely careful.'

.Bone-marrow transplants are risky and delicate operations which first became regular practice in 1970. Bone-marrow replaces billions of blood cells that die every day. If the marrow is badly damaged, it cannot produce enough cells to fight off infections and, in that sense, the effect of radiation can be compared to that of some leukaemias and to AIDS. Fortunately, bone-marrow has a remarkable capacity for regeneration. But a transplant may be the only survival option open for those who receive a dose as high as 300 rems of radiation. A syringe is used to extract the gelatinous marrow from a donor's pelvis. Fat and bone fragments are removed and the marrow is purified to guard against rejection by mixing it with the soybean extract, lectin — a technique developed by the Israeli biophysicist Yair Reisner. It is then injected into the veins to find its way to the marrow spaces in the bone.

Gale insisted that Reisner himself should join the Moscow team because he 'intended to bring in the best people in the world'. The Soviet Union had broken off diplomatic relations with Israel after the 1967 Middle East War. Under these circumstances, however, the Soviet authorities did not hesitate to co-operate, as they had not hesitated over accepting Gale's own offer of help despite their hostilities with official Washington.

The day he arrived in Moscow, Gale rang Reisner, who was by chance visiting New York for a symposium. There is reputed to be only one direct-dial international telephone in the whole of Moscow — and it is in the office of Armand Hammer's Occidental Oil.

'I was pretty surprised to hear from Bob Gale,' Reisner recalled later. 'We're in two competing groups normally — he's in the Californian group, I'm in the New York group.' (Reisner had spent three years in New York, from 1978–81, before returning to his post at the Weizmann Institute of Science biophysics department at Rehovat, south of Tel Aviv.) 'He asked me if I could come over to help, and said he'd already checked with the authorities that there would be no problems about the fact that I was an Israeli.' Gale warned him that he would find virtually nothing in Moscow. The Russians had started to perform bone-marrow transplants only the previous year and had carried out no more than 10 at the time of Chernobyl. Nine of the 10 patients had died. In the west, by comparison, more than 9,000 such operations have been performed in the last 15 years — at the Sloan Kettering research centre in New York alone they perform three a week.

'I told him I'd come on condition he promised to be at the airport to meet me just in case.' Reisner spent the weekend amassing $40,000-worth of equipment. Armand Hammer footed the bill and arranged first-class travel from Israel via Frankfurt.

Reisner recalls:

> I was immediately taken to the airport VIP room for a drink. Gale was very tired indeed and very worried. He fell asleep in the car as we drove straight to Hospital No. 6.

It took the Israeli a full day to unpack the 16 crates of equipment he had brought with him, and by the time he was ready to start, three of the seven patients Gale had lined up for him had already died. 'The patients were all young men — technicians, firemen, a doctor who had rushed to the plant and a guard,' Reisner says. 'They had severe third-degree burns and had received radiation doses of between 700—1,000 rems.'

Reisner's skills were especially needed since his pioneering work, for which he received the British Sir Charles Clore prize in 1983, was in the field of transplanting from unmatched donors. It is essential to match the donor's and the patient's blood-types perfectly. Otherwise the recipient can reject the marrow, or the marrow can reject the recipient. Relatives from all over Russia had been flown to Moscow as donors. Six victims were so heavily irradiated that they did not have enough blood left for accurate matching, and the technique tried was exotic. Primitive blood-forming cells were taken from the deep-frozen livers of aborted 3—4-month-old foetuses: injected, this tissue appears to form blood cells just like marrow.

The team commandeered drugs and materials from all over the world: Gale estimates that about 15 countries were involved. Armand Hammer paid a total bill of $600,000 — his own estimate — as a free gift to the Soviet Union. The first transplant was performed on the Thursday, and then one more each day thereafter. After a 16-hour day, the foreign doctors slumped asleep at the VIP Hotel Sovietskaya. Reisner said at the time:

> Everyone had high praise for the Soviet doctors. They were very intelligent, very decisive — they didn't fool around . . . You do your best, but you're playing against very bad odds. It'll be a great miracle if any of our patients survives.

Gale was more bullish. Writing on September 7th, he boasted: 'In time we got the Russians to think like American businessmen. We said "Nothing is impossible".' Working in shifts, the doctors eventually performed 13 transplants. Gale was not slow to claim the credit. 'We managed to save five through our efforts,' he said, 'which made it all worthwhile.' He told us that a success-rate of more than 30 per cent was better than his previous average of 25 per cent.

But the Russian official report to the IAEA made it clear they thought Gale's treatment actually did more harm than good. They credited him with only four survivors, who, they believe, would have lived anyway, and whom the transplants actually made worse. Indeed, the report says, the interventions may have helped to kill two patients who would otherwise have survived.

Gale's patients were trapped in a difficult medical paradox. Seven of them were so badly irradiated that the immune system did not reject the transplanted marrow. But the radiation killed them from skin and intestinal damage before the transplant could take effect. The other six had received lower doses and therefore had a chance of survival: but this meant they were well enough to reject the transplanted marrow, and the process of rejection seems to have worsened their condition. In such cases, says the report, the transplants will 'always have a negative effect in therapeutic terms and even endanger life as a result of the high risk of secondary disease developing'. In the two of the six who perished, this 'may have contributed to death'.

The report says, with dry understatement: 'In general, it can be said that bone-marrow transplants were not a decisive factor in treatment after this particular accident.' In Vienna, Academician Leonid Ilyin, vice-president of the USSR academy of medical sciences and director of the Institute of Biophysics, dismissed media acclaim of the transplants as 'profoundly faulty'. Most of the western experts at the conference agreed that the technique seemed to have little future in treating radiation injuries of this type.

Most of the 203 people diagnosed as having acute radiation sickness were cured, in the words of Dr Roger Berry of London's Middlesex Hospital, a conference delegate, 'by good conventional medicine'. Conditions had to be improvised. There were not enough sterile intensive-care units. So the Russian doctors took over several hospital wards and used simple ultra-violet lights — like those used for killing flies — to sterilise the air. The contrast with Dr Gale's flying circus could not have been more marked. By the end of August, the 31 'prompt' victims had died. Thirty more were still in hospital, but expected to live.

The Chernobyl accident has clearly shown the limitations of medicine after nuclear disasters. A tremendous international effort failed to save more than a handful of the most severely irradiated victims, and Oleg Shchepin, the Soviet Union's first deputy health minister, admitted that the accident had revealed a shortage of good Russian doctors experienced in such treatment. If weather conditions had been different and thousands had been seriously irradiated, little could have been done to help them. What if the world's next reactor accident occurs in less fortuitous circumstances? And what if there is nuclear war?

The dramas of Municipal Hospital No. 6 were, of course, only the first act in a medical tragedy that will run, at the very least, for several decades. In the immediate aftermath of the accident, the Poles, typically, greeted the original Russian casualty announcements with a wry joke. St Peter, they said, went to the Pearly Gates and saw a large throng pushing and shoving to get in. 'What's all this?' he demanded. 'In the communiqué, they only mentioned two!'

The throng may arrive more slowly than the joke foresaw, but they will, inevitably, turn up. The later waves of death are much more subtle and will affect many more people. They also take very much longer to strike. It will be a couple of years before the first leukaemias caused by radiation from Chernobyl appear, and several more before they reach their peak. Just as this wave begins to die away, the first of the other cancers will appear, and their numbers will go on increasing for 40 years or more.

These leukaemias and other cancers will strike all over the western Soviet Union and the rest of Europe. For while it takes a dose of 100 rems or more to induce acute radiation sickness, there is no such threshold for cancers. Scientists assume that even the smallest dose of radiation could be enough.

No-one will ever know the exact cancer toll. The Chernobyl cancers will be scattered among a population in which millions die from identical tumours anyway. So in the absense of hard data, scientists have had to resort to rough rules of thumb. For a start, nobody knows exactly how much radioactive material there was in the core of reactor No. 4 at 1.23 a.m. on that fateful morning. Figures in the official Russian report to the IAEA suggest that it may have contained a grand total of 52,857,000,000,000,000,000 bq. of radioactivity — give or take a few quintillion bq. But this remains only a guess. Nor do we know how much of it poured out of the reactor during the 10 days it took to bring it under control. The Russian report puts the 'total release of fission products' as about 3.5 per cent. But this specifically omits radioactive inert gases, especially xenon-133. Western experts conclude there have been other underestimates, particularly of radioactive iodine and caesium, and estimate a total figure of about 10 per cent. This coincides with early, private Russian estimates. But we will never know for sure. Some clues have been dispersed around the world. The rest lie entombed in the core's concrete burial-pit.

There has also been considerable confusion, to put it mildly, about the levels of contamination around the reactor. In the month after the accident, the Soviet authorities issued ludicrously low figures, presumably in an ill-judged attempt to minimise its public impact. Time after time during May, senior Soviet officials insisted in public that the highest levels of radiation found at the plant after the accident were of the order of 15—30 millirems an hour.

The official Russian report to the IAEA comes nearer to the truth, but not much. It gingerly admits that 'radiation levels near the plant exceeded 100 millirems an hour'. It took an unscripted aside by Victor Legasov, during his August presentation of the report, finally to inform the world. Levels near the plant, he said, were initially of the order of hundreds of thousands of rems an hour — in other words, millions of times higher than the numbers given in the report. Indeed, he said, the levels had been so high that they had not been able to find equipment anywhere in the world that was capable of measuring them. One reason for these astronomic levels was that the fragmented fuel, flung high into the air by the explosion, was so heavy that it rained down again on the reactor site in a deadly hail. In Pripyat, some miles away, levels reached 1,000 millirems an hour in the Kurchatov St area — the one nearest the plant — at 5 p.m. on April 27, just after the evacuation.

The Soviet authorities have been similarly coy about the individual radiation doses received by the two groups of evacuees. But during close questioning at Vienna, western experts extracted the fact that thousands of people have in fact received external doses of 30—50 rems, while Dr Gale says 25,000 received 40—50 rems. In other words these people — most of whom, though the Russians do not explicitly admit it, came from the area not evacuated until 9 days after the accident — received about half the dose needed to bring on acute radiation sickness. The Russians refused point-blank to say how many pregnant women were evacuated (there must have been many hundreds). Leading international experts believe that they were all forced to have abortions.

In the aftermath of the accident, the Russians certainly tried to play down the doses received by the people in Kiev, the nearest big city to the evacuation area. Boris Semenov said at the IAEA in May that the maximum dose received in Kiev would, if sustained over a whole month, amount to no more than a single X-ray (Soviet TV gave even lower estimates). Yet tests carried out at an American nuclear power plant on tourists who had briefly visited the city two days after the accident showed that 14 of them had absorbed 50 times as much radiation as from a chest X-ray. Certainly, the two million citizens of Kiev came to have little faith in the official assurances. Soviet TV showed films of British students who had been studying in the city leaving the country. The idea was to make fun of panicky foreigners. However, the amused viewers were alarmed to see that the students were required to change out of their clothes and put on tracksuits before they were allowed on the plane. (Some of the clothes were later found to be so contaminated that they were confiscated by the British radiation authorities.)

Then, more than a week after the accident began, the Ukrainian Ministry of Health suddenly started broadcasting instructions against eating leafy vegetables and allowing children out of doors for long periods. Further warnings followed. Residents were warned to wash themselves and their homes regularly, to stop drinking alcohol, to stop smoking, and to prevent their children from playing on the ground. A ban was imposed on street sales of ice-cream, cakes and drinks. By now many citizens were not waiting to hear any more, or at least making sure that they evacuated their children. They started packing the trains to Moscow. Long queues built up at the ticket office at Kiev station. Train after overcrowded train pulled in to the capital with at least 70 per cent of their seats filled by unaccompanied children. One elderly woman arriving with her daughter and two grandchildren said: 'There is no question of keeping children in Kiev a moment longer, the risk is too great. Every mother that I know wants to get her children away.' Finally, the authorities gave in, closed elementary schools and kindergartens for the holidays ten days early, and sent 250,000 children out of the city to summer camps.

The citizens had good reason to be worried. The authorities had arbitrarily increased the maximum permitted dose in the city to 10 rems a year, 20 times the upper limits allowed under international regulations. And the British National Radiological Protection Board carried out tests on vegetables smuggled out of Kiev after the accident — and recorded measurements of up to 1,300,000 bq. per kgm, 13 times the level at which food should have been destroyed.

Indeed, the Soviet authorities seem to have been remarkably slow and ineffectual in controlling contaminated food both near Chernobyl and throughout the country. Officially the authorities banned the consumption of milk within the 30 km zone from early in the morning of May 1st. This was several days late, and, as they now admit, was disregarded. The 90,000 people left in the area went on drinking local milk up to their evacuation on May 4th and 5th, greatly adding to their radiation doses. Some received doses of hundreds of rems of iodine-131 to their thyroids. Even further afield, in the central Ukraine and south-east and north-west Byelorussia, milk contained many hundreds of times the permitted level. Though the Russians say that centralised sales were strictly controlled, they admit that rural people will have consumed this highly contaminated milk. Even more seriously, the authorities did not get around to controlling other radionuclides and other foods until the end of May, though evidence had been flooding in for weeks of serious contamination far from the accident site. In

Gomelskaya in Byelorussia, for example, 40 per cent of the meat, 30 per cent of the milk and milk products, 15 per cent of the green vegetables, and 90 per cent of the fish exceeded radiation standards. Since the accident, food contaminated with radioactive caesium has been eaten all over European Russia — and this will be the main source of the tens of thousands of cancer deaths now expected to take place over the next decades as a result of Chernobyl.

Radiation doses to the people of Europe outside the Soviet Union, though very much lower, are also hard to estimate. There were worrying indications that some governments — even in western Europe — were also reluctant to release information. For example, the French government — the most fanatically pro-nuclear outside the Soviet Union — had lied for a week about the levels of radiation from Chernobyl that had reached its territory. Asked why he had withheld the information that some levels were up to 400 times normal, Pierre Pellerin, director of the Service for Radiation Protection, opined, 'Quite simply because there were two holidays in two weeks and it was very complicated to transmit the data.' Meanwhile in Britain the Ministry of Agriculture insisted on publishing *average* levels of radiation in milk, concealing the much higher levels in parts of the country, like the north-west.

Even where the levels have been accurately recorded and honestly reported, it will be hard to work out how much people have been affected. This is because the radioactive fall-out from the cloud was spread very unevenly across Europe, depending almost entirely on where it rained. The evidence of this can be seen most dramatically in Sweden, where the authorities promptly set out to map radiation levels across the country. They found that most of Sweden was little affected, but there was an extraordinary hot-spot of radiation over a large area of countryside south of Gayle about 150 km (90 miles) north of Stockholm. Over this area, levels of caesium-137 reached 137,000 bq. per square metre. This means that, in the immediate aftermath of Chernobyl, 27 times as much of the long-lived radionuclide in rain fell on the area than it received during the entire 40-year programme of nuclear weapons testing. In parts of Bavaria, levels of Chernobyl fall-out were found to be 30—40 times those received from all the weapons tests.

Similar rainfall hot-spots were found all over Europe. One of the worst had been identified in north-east Poland; around the town of Mikolajki, for example, radiation levels reached at least 500 times normal. In parts of East Germany they were 100 times normal. Levels of caesium-137, also 100 times above normal, were even found in the English Lake District.

This poses a unique problem for the scientists trying to work out cancer casualty levels. Normally they are used to working out global figures from such sources as bomb testing, which blast radioactive materials so high into the troposphere that they fall out fairly evenly over the northern hemisphere. Here, with such wide variations, they have no alternative but to get down, literally, to the grass roots, measure radiation levels all over Europe and work out how many people live in the affected areas, before they even start to do their sums. In mid-May, some of the world's leading authorities on radiation began, under United Nations auspices, to piece the clues together. But it will be two years, at least, before they come up with their first figures.

In the meantime, the best evidence we have comes from technical annex 7 of the Soviet report to the August IAEA conference. This contained some detailed, if preliminary, estimates of the radiation doses received by the 75 million people of European Russia. These total some 240,000,000 man rem over the next 50 to 70 years. Almost ninety per cent of this dose would be the result of eating food contaminated with caesium-137. As luck would have it, crops incorporate the radionuclide 10 to 100 times more efficiently from the light Poles'ye soil of parts of the Ukraine and Byelorussia — the Soviet Union's breadbasket — than they do from normal soils.

Using internationally accepted conversion formulas, it is possible to calculate that 30,000 to 50,000 people are likely to die of cancer in European Russia, depending on which formula is used. The Russians' own estimates appear, from evidence in their technical annex, to be around the middle of that range. Even the most conservative scientists accept these current estimates. They are about 10 times as high as the same scientists expected immediately after the disaster and would, indeed, make Chernobyl the worst man-made accident in the world in terms of deaths alone.

But this is far from being the last word. Some leading authorities say that the figures are far too low because they are based on the old Hiroshima data. These, as we have seen, many believe to be hopelessly inadequate. Such scientists estimate that there will be some 250,000 cancer deaths. Others argue that no more than a couple of thousand deaths can realistically be expected. Indeed, as the IAEA autumn conference progressed, and predictions of tens of thousands of deaths appeared in the world's press, conference officials made increasingly frantic attempts to revise the figures downward at press conferences.

So far there is less evidence to be found in most countries outside the Soviet Union, though some national authorities have come out with their own rough estimates. A Polish government team predicted at the beginning of May that between 200 and 500 of their own countrymen would die from cancer as a result of Chernobyl over the next 30 years. In Sweden, leading scientists were estimating between 100 and 150 fatalities. Even in distant Britain, official estimates suggested that some 45 people would die, which means that the Chernobyl disaster 3,000 km (1,850 miles) away would take a higher toll in Britain than even the domestic Windscale nuclear plant fire of 1957. Critics would again multiply these figures severalfold. Professor Edward Radford, one of the world's leading authorities, made a preliminary prediction of some 3,000 cancer deaths in all western European countries.

Of course these cancers will be spread out in a population of scores of millions, one-third of whom will develop cancer anyway for other reasons. The lower the radiation dose, the most thinly the cancers will be spread.

If it is going to be hard to work out the cancer toll from Chernobyl, it will be well-nigh impossible to estimate its effects on future generations. Radiation damages genetic material, and can therefore lead to offspring being born with genetic disease. Sometimes the damage may lie dormant for generations, and only surface in the descendants of people who have been dead for centuries. Unfortunately, the human evidence for the extent of genetic damage is almost non-existent. The Hiroshima studies have turned up only two probable mutations in the children of survivors. But evidence from animals is unequivocal that genetic damage does occur, and there is no reason to suppose that humans are immune. Indeed, detectable chromosome damage has been found in people exposed to remarkably low levels of radiation, though its significance is unknown. In the absence of proper human data scientists construct complicated formulae based on animal tests to work out the likely damage to man. For what it is worth, the United Nations Scientific Committee on the Effects of Atomic Radiation reckons that a general dose of 100 rem will produce about 2,000 serious mutations and genetic diseases in every million live births in the first generation after exposure, and an ultimate figure of 15,000 for every million live births if the exposure continues at the same rate over the generations.

However, it is just possible that Chernobyl may eventually yield some answers both about the accident's toll of death and disease and about the true dangers of radiation. The Soviet Union has promised to study the 135,000 people evacuated from the 30 km zone. The study will be larger than the research carried out at Hiroshima. Scientists believe that it is likely to be more reliable because this time measurements have been taken of the doses received by many thousands of the most exposed people. 'The human experiment has now been done,' says one top British specialist. 'At last we can test our hypotheses.'

As they began to realise the size of the research opportunity, scientists from all over the world began to scramble to get a slice of the action. First in the field was again Dr Gale, who began to speak of the possibilities even as he was completing his transplant work. Two days after the August IAEA conference ended, he flew back to Moscow to try to set up the study. He left behind an angry community of radiation scientists. 'I shall be gravely alarmed if Dr Gale does the work,' said Dr John Dunster, Director of Britain's National Radiological Protection Board, 'and so will most of my colleagues.'

Whoever does the work, the human guinea pigs are, in Dr Dunster's words, 'going to have a hell of a time for the rest of their lives', subject to constant, searching examinations. 'Every damn year these people are going to be taken to pieces and put together again,' he says.

The cloud of fall-out was only part of the radiation problem.

At Chernobyl, the emergency teams faced an Augean stables. The Russians seemed confident that they could succeed in decontaminating the nuclear wasteland around the plant, and fulfil Gorbachev's instructions that 'the area must be restored to the state that is absolutely safe for the health and normal life of people'.

Some leading western authorities believe they can do it, if they spend enough time and money. But most are profoundly doubtful. Dr Dunster says that laboratory experiments indicate that such decontamination is 'quite remarkably difficult', and it is likely to be even more so in the field. In the presumably easier conditions of Three Mile Island, it was originally thought that the power station could be decontaminated in two years at a cost of $200 million. Seven years and $1,000 million later, the problems still seem insurmountable. You can scrub concrete apparently clean, only to find it recontaminating itself, seemingly from radioactive materials escaping from the interior to the surface.

The Soviet Union seems anxious to get the area back to normal, to get the evacuees back to their homes, to restart the remaining three power stations at Chernobyl and complete building the other two. There is a large industrial and agricultural investment at stake — and an enormous amount of national pride. This has led some sober western experts to develop a dark suspicion. In their determination to be seen to have done a good job, and to play down the effects of the accident, might the Russians not be prepared to reactivate the area and to move the people back even if they have little success with decontamination? To be sure, many of the evacuees would develop cancer, but the bulk of the disease would not become evident for 20 or 30 years, by which time the present leaders would long be dead. The immediate political cost might be very small; the gain to prestige from 'solving' the problem would be enormous.

One of the reactors was, in fact, re-started at Chernobyl in October 1986. Furthermore, the chairman of the state committee for environment control told Soviet TV viewers: 'We are thinking about how to use this land in future in the interests of the national economy and agriculture.' It is hard to find anyone, except it appears in the Soviet Union, who thinks that the land in the exclusion zone will be fit for agriculture for many years to come.

Both harvesting contaminated crops and allowing a premature return to the evacuation zone would greatly increase the scale of the Chernobyl tragedy.

It is doubtful whether the exact final extent of the radiological disaster will ever be known. Everyone in a position to know the truth has an interest in playing down the effects of the accident in the interests of further nuclear growth worldwide.

Partly because of the human factor, senior figures at both the U.S. Nuclear Regulatory Commission and the IAEA privately believe that we can expect a major reactor accident every decade. And some are already going further and saying openly that this might not be so dreadful, after all. Dr Morris Rosen, the Director of Nuclear Safety at the IAEA, speculated openly at the Vienna post-mortem that the health effects of a Chernobyl every decade, even of one every year, might be thought 'acceptable'. And in Canada Professor Jovan Jovanovich of the University of Manitoba predicted that within 30 years an accident like Chernobyl or Three Mile Island might be happening every year. 'We will get used to them, and newspapers will report them on page 37,' he added. 'Nuclear power is here to stay. In fact, we need a lot more of it.' Legasov in his closing address to the Vienna conference did not regard the issue quite so blandly: 'Russian scientists are very frightened that the Chernobyl accident will lead to the abolition of nuclear energy,' he said. 'From humankind's point of view, that would be a tragic error.'

10 End of the nuclear dream

'Our technology has outpaced our understanding, our cleverness has grown faster than our wisdom.'
Dr Roger Revelle, chairman of the US national committee for the International Biological Program

After the Chernobyl disaster, the world's nuclear industry faces a crisis of confidence. As worried populations throughout both eastern and western Europe listened anxiously to radio and television advice about how to avoid the worst effects of the cloud of radioactivity which swept over them, another group of people was even more concerned – the nuclear salesmen. Anxiety about the future of their product is not new to this particular group of men, who have experienced more ups and downs in public esteem than the average roller-coaster. Previous setbacks have already come close to crippling the industry in its most important market, the United States, and have damaged it everywhere. But no previous incident has had half the international impact of the Chernobyl disaster. Can nuclear power survive? Does it deserve to? And if the world is to manage without nuclear power, what other sources can provide the electricity to keep the lights burning into the twenty-first century?

The nuclear industry and its powerful supporters in government would say such questions could only be asked by the technically illiterate or those blinded by environmentalism and hatred for high technology. To them it appears both inevitable and good that more nuclear stations should be built. To fail to do so, as one of them wrote to the *Observer* after the Chernobyl disaster, would be to condemn future generations to darkness and death. Such technological arrogance has been bred by a generation in which nuclear power has been isolated from real public pressure, and has developed in a close and unhealthy symbiosis with central government.

For forty years nuclear power has been shamelessly pampered by governments of every colour in almost every developed country. It has been given the best brains and the biggest budgets governments could provide. The laws of economics have been repealed in its favour, while its environmental hazards have been politely overlooked. Only the defence industries have enjoyed a longer or a more luxurious free ride. Yet at the end of this, the industry in most of the western world is unprofitable, depressed and demoralized. In the Soviet Union it has just suffered a catastrophic accident. It is a history that calls for little explanation.

It began in the aftermath of the Manhattan Project. Many of those who had taken part felt horror and something close to shame at what had been done. The destruction of Hiroshima and Nagasaki and, worse still, the race to build a 'super-bomb' yet more devastating in its effects left many physicists disillusioned. It was no consolation to them that once the feasibility of a nuclear fission bomb had become clear there was no possible way of preventing its development, if not by the Allies then by Germany under Adolf Hitler. They felt that a beautiful science had been irretrievably soiled by what had happened in Los Alamos between 1941 and 1945, and what might yet happen to the world if nuclear weapons could not be controlled.

To such people, and to the politicians who were responsible for directing them, it was a moral imperative to find a positive side to nuclear fission. Initially it was believed that prospects for nuclear power generation would be limited by a shortage of uranium, but the demands of the bomb programme soon established sufficient supplies of the metal, so that obstacle was soon out of the way. By the early 1950s enthusiasm for nuclear electricity was growing, and series of absurdly optimistic plans were drawn up. None of them was realized. The British plan, launched in 1955, was trebled in 1957 and revoked two years later. Soviet estimates in the 1956 Five Year Plan simply disappeared without trace, while the German plan of 1957 to build five reactors produced just one and the Japanese 'long-term plan' of 1957 produced no plants at all. It was the first example of optimism being crushed by experience, something which has become all too familiar in the succeeding years.

The second half of the 1950s also saw the two worst nuclear accidents before Chernobyl – the Windscale fire of 1957 and the disastrous release of radioactivity from nuclear waste in the Soviet Union in late 1957 or early 1958. While these accidents were a sobering experience, they did not have a significant effect on confidence. In Britain the authorities were able to persuade the public that the fire had been an isolated incident that would not happen again, while the Soviet authorities simply kept their own disaster secret until it came to light in the article written almost twenty years later by a Soviet scientist living in the west, Zhores Medvedev (see chapter 4).

By the early 1960s optimism was back in charge. The turning point came in 1963, with the contract to build the Oyster Creek plant (see chapter 3). It began a stampede into nuclear power by the American utilities. During 1966 and 1967, they ordered 51 nuclear plants, all of them on cost-plus contracts that shifted the burden of any cost overruns away from the contractors and on to the utilities. It was a bandwagon on to which almost everybody jumped, though many were later to regret their impetuosity.

In Britain, a similar rush of blood to the head produced

different results – the AGR disaster. In 1965 it was decided to carry out a direct comparison of the generating costs of an American-style light water reactor and an advanced gas-cooled reactor of British design. To nobody's astonishment – for this has always been a deeply nationalistic industry – the AGR emerged on top. 'The greatest breakthrough of all time', the Minister of Power called it. In fact, it was probably the worst decision ever made in an industry which has never been noted for sober judgment.

The result of the appraisal was to give the AGR an advantage of just one-hundredth of a penny per kilowatt hour generated, a margin so slim that it was absurd even to cite it. It needed only a tiny shift in material prices, a delay in construction, an engineering error, or a strike, to blow such spuriously precise figures out of the water. At Dungeness in Kent, where the first AGR was begun, all these happened, and more.

Originally quoted at a price of £89 million, for completion by 1970, the Dungeness AGR eventually produced its first electricity in 1983, at a total cost of £600 million. Almost everything that could go wrong did go wrong. 'It was a bad buy,' Mr John Baker, a member of the CEGB, has admitted. 'It would have been better if we hadn't built it, but we can't rewrite history now.'

Nuclear optimists in the United States suffered many similar setbacks. The Diablo Canyon station in California, originally budgeted at $450 million, ultimately cost $4.4 billion. In Indiana, the Public Service Company budgeted $1.4 billion for its 2,260 megawatt plant at Marble Hill, but had already spent $2.5 billion to bring the plant half-way to completion when it gave up and abandoned construction. The Midland, Michigan, plant was launched in 1969 by Consumers Power Co., with a price tag of $267 million. By 1984 it was still only 85 per cent complete and had cost $3.4 billion.

The Soviet Union, too, had difficulties producing its nuclear plants on time and to a tight budget. At Khmelnitskii, for example, where many of the construction workers are Poles, and the plant is designed to export electricity to Eastern Europe, construction is still not complete although it began in 1977. By western standards this is not too bad, and some Soviet stations have been built at extraordinary speed – at Zaporozhe workers claimed a world record after commissioning a 1,000 megawatt station in only four years, and nine months. How many corners were cut to achieve this result, of course, we do not know. There has been strong criticism within the Soviet Union of the standards of construction of some nuclear power stations.

In general, despite successes such as Zaporozhe, the Soviet Union appears to have suffered the same problems as everybody else. In 1980 the central plan projected the construction of 25,000 megawatts of nuclear capacity by 1985, but in fact only 15,800 megawatts was achieved.

In spite of success stories like the French programme, where reactors were built rapidly and on time, nuclear power has often proved an expensive embarrassment. Far from providing low-cost power, many of the plants have had a disastrous history, plunging their builders into the economic morass. Even the increases in the price of oil that hit the world in 1973 and 1979 were no real help. Although they made nuclear power seem attractive in the short term, they had two other effects which were much less helpful. They helped to create a raging inflation which put up the cost of building the plants, further damaging their economic viability, and they depressed the world economy so substantially that electricity demand fell. The end result was to damage nuclear power's prospects, at least in the short and medium term.

Since the mid-1970s, many more nuclear plants have been cancelled than have been ordered. In the United States, 11 plants were cancelled in 1975 and another 31 in the next three years. Was this simply, as analysts suggested, a temporary correction in the market? Apparently not: 16 plants were scrapped in 1980, 6 in 1981 and another 18 in 1982. Between 1975 and 1983, 87 nuclear plants were cancelled in the United States, totalling 83,000 megawatts. Over the same period 58,000 megawatts of coal-fired plants were ordered.

Utility managers were bewildered at the trend, and some felt a sense of betrayal. 'The first lesson we've learned is "Don't build nuclear plants in America",' one of them commented in 1984. 'You subject yourself to financial risk and public abuse.' Hugh Parris, Manager of Power at the Tennessee Valley Authority, which made a massive commitment to nuclear power plants in the 1960s only to abandon most of them at a $1.8 billion loss and return to coal-fired stations, said: 'We recognized the situation we were in and took the most prudent action. Some folks might look at abandoned nuclear plants as monuments to mistakes and stupidity. I look at them as monuments to good management.'

Britain did no better over the same period. The series of abrupt policy reversals which have been a feature of British nuclear policy-making continued, and became even more frenzied. In 1974 Sir Arthur Hawkins, then Chairman of the CEGB, astonished everybody by declaring that he wished to build no fewer than 18 PWRs. Not only was this a programme far greater than any previously contemplated in Britain, but it would have employed a type of reactor not yet licensed for use. Not a single one of Sir Arthur's 18 plants has been built, yet the CEGB has over most of the subsequent period had a huge plant reserve and has been able to mothball several almost new oil-fired plants for long periods, and close down many smaller coal-fired plants.

In West Germany, ambitious plans for 45,000 megawatts of installed nuclear capacity by 1990 have had to be scaled down, and many plants ordered before 1975 have never been built because of falling electricity growth rates and the success of opponents in licensing hearings. In Sweden, where anti-nuclear sentiments are particularly strong, the referendum held in 1980 voted in favour of stopping the nuclear programme and phasing out nuclear power by 2010.

In the wake of the Chernobyl accident, the mood has moved even more decisively against nuclear power – at least among those who admitted to having any doubts before. The Austrian Chancellor, Dr Fred Sinowatz, announced that Austria's only nuclear plant, at Zwentendorf, completed in 1978 but never used because a referendum decided against commissioning it, will now be taken apart. Dismantling Zwentendorf was a necessary consequence of Chernobyl, Sinowatz told parliament. 'The problem of the use of nuclear energy in Austria can be considered as decided and closed,' he said.

Another quick cancellation was announced in the Philippines by President Cory Aquino. She said that her government would mothball an almost completed reactor being built on the Bataan peninsula at a cost of $2.1 billion.

In Yugoslavia, too, the Chernobyl accident had immediate effects. The authorities dropped, without explanation, plans to build the country's second nuclear station at Prevlaka. Although there was no official confirmation that the cancellation was in response to Chernobyl, the political weekly *NIN* reported that as the reason.

In the Netherlands, where two nuclear plants are operating, the government was obliged to abandon plans for a major expansion of nuclear power in the 1990s. An opinion poll held two weeks after the Chernobyl accident, while the radioactive cloud was still wandering about over Europe, showed that 70 per cent of those questioned in the Netherlands were opposed to nuclear power. In West Germany, a poll in *Der Spiegel* produced almost identical results, with 69 per cent opposed to any new plants, and 54 per cent believing that the existing plants, which provide one-third of West Germany's electricity, should be phased out.

The evidence is that Chernobyl has fallen like a hammer-blow on an industry that was already groggy. The poor economic performance of many plants, combined with public disquiet and a relatively slow growth in electricity demand, has conspired to overturn all the ambitious predictions made a decade ago. Those who built nuclear plants during that period, like the French, have saddled their utilities with large debts and excess capacity. Those who failed to build the plants they promised have lost face, but little else; electricity demand has been so sluggish that they have had no difficulty in meeting it from other sources.

Even the most determinedly pro-nuclear nations will find their programmes much harder to follow since Chernobyl's plumes darkened the skies of Europe. For one thing, nuclear power throughout the world must now become much more expensive. 'After the Three Mile Island accident, worldwide output from pressurized water reactors fell by 15 per cent because reactor managers felt they had to reduce power output to "play safe",' says Colin Sweet, director of London's Centre for Energy Studies. 'In addition, costs rose because regulatory bodies piled on safety requirements that increased power-production costs. When one reactor goes wrong, there is always a knock-on effect.'

Sweet's analysis indicates that whatever the nuclear enthusiasts may say, accidents do affect the industry. Officially, accidents are always things that happen to other people. Once they have happened, and the spokesmen are forced to explain them, two arguments are generally deployed: the accident was nothing like as bad as the media claimed, and it couldn't happen here.

After the Windscale fire, for example, the public was told, 'There was not a large amount of radioactivity released. The amount was not hazardous and, in fact, it was carried out to sea by the wind.' (None of this was true.) After Chernobyl, the Soviet spokesmen concentrated on denunciations of the western media for exaggerating the accident, while western spokesmen fell back on 'It couldn't happen here'. The evidence is, however, that the public finds such protestations unconvincing. Most people recognize intuitively what many nuclear spokesmen are reluctant to admit: that nuclear power stations, like all complex machines, have the ability to fail, sometimes in ways which their designers had not anticipated. In reality, of course, nuclear engineers know very well that sub-systems within their plants can and will fail. But they behave as if this knowledge were too dangerous for the public to be told.

The history of technology is littered with examples of new machines failing catastrophically. Those who developed the early steam engines in the eighteenth century risked their lives every day from boiler explosions. When the railways came along to make use of steam power, derailments, axle breakages, bridge collapses and signalling failures, all claimed further lives. But the engineers learned slowly through their mistakes, eventually producing in the modern railway the safest form of transport known to man. During the twentieth century an exactly similar process has taken place in the development of aircraft and, more recently, spacecraft. It can be argued, without straining for paradox, that the history of technology is a history of disasters, each leading to better and safer machinery.

The problem is that nuclear power poses dangers on an altogether larger scale, so that the time-honoured method of learning by mistakes cannot be safely applied. The potential disasters no longer affect a few people directly concerned with the technology (as do accidents in coal mines, for example) but may affect thousands whose only link with nuclear power is to live close to a power station. These involuntary victims have made no careful calculation of whether the benefit they gain from nuclear power exceeds the risks they face. They lack the data to make such a calculation and have no way of stopping the plant being built if they decide the risks are too great. They have to contract out these decisions to others whose interests are different and whose assessments of costs and benefits are different – the utilities, the Departments of Energy and the nuclear engineering companies.

None the less, there are circumstances in which public anxieties about nuclear power can be effective. A rough rule of thumb seems to apply: the larger the utility, the more difficult it is to influence its decisions.

Nationalized generating boards like those of Britain and France can write their own tickets, backed by central government. Where utilities are smaller and in the private sector, as in the United States, they are much more responsive to public pressure. While the decline of the atom in the United States is largely the result of the poor economic figures, environmental pressure has also had significant effects. Utility presidents simply do not want to go to war with their own consumers to force through an unwelcome nuclear plant. In Britain the opposition is usually focused on a lengthy public inquiry in which opponents are allowed to make their case. Such inquiries provide a forum for opponents, but pose no insuperable problems for the industry except delay. No public inquiry has ever ruled against a nuclear development, and nobody seriously expects Sir Frank Layfield, QC, to do so when he produces his report towards the end of 1986 on the plans to build a PWR at Sizewell in Suffolk.

For many opponents, of course, it is the close links between nuclear power and nuclear weapons – particularly close in the case of Chernobyl – which provide the clinching arguments. Nuclear power stations in Britain, the United States and the Soviet Union developed from the first nuclear 'piles' for producing plutonium. At Chernobyl, the development did not go very far, since the design is clearly adaptable for either power or plutonium production. But any nuclear plant, whatever its design, can be used for producing plutonium, as the Canadians discovered when India used a small reactor supplied by them to produce its first atom bomb.

The dilemma faced by western governments, and particularly the nuclear weapons states, is how to protect their nuclear exports from similar misuse. Great efforts have been made over many years to develop a foolproof system, but few critics are satisfied. The International Atomic Energy Agency in Vienna, the body charged with examining nuclear reactors to ensure material is not being diverted for military purposes, is effective only so long as nobody begins to misbehave. It possesses no real sanctions, has too few inspectors to provide an absolute assurance, and can do little if a nation closes the doors to its inspectors.

Aware of these defects, the major nuclear nations got together during the 1970s to form the London Nuclear Suppliers Club, a group pledged to control the export of sensitive technologies to countries which might have nuclear ambitions. At the time, the principal anxiety was in Latin America, where Brazil and Argentina were under military rule and pursuing ambitious nuclear power programmes. Since then democracy has been restored in both countries, relations between them have improved, and the economic slump has slowed their nuclear programmes.

Although the immediate worries may have subsided, the issue has not gone away. There are still plenty of nations in the world which would like the opportunity to develop nuclear weapons, and several that are doing so already. Pakistan is expected to be the next to test a bomb, and

India has revived its own weapons programme, largely dormant since the first explosion, so that it can match its neighbour. In the Middle East are several regimes who would like a bomb to use as the ultimate threat against Israel, which already has nuclear weapons of its own as a defence of last resort. Israel has never actually tested a weapon (or has not admitted to doing so) but nobody doubts that it has the knowledge and the materials to assemble several weapons if the need arose.

Since the late 1970s a lot of diplomatic pressure has been employed to try to persuade six key states to sign the nuclear Non-Proliferation Treaty (NPT) – India, Pakistan, Israel, South Africa, Argentina and Brazil. None has shown any inclination to do so, for reasons which are logical, consistent and hard to fault. They argue, first, that the NPT is a discriminatory treaty which permits three members – the United States, the United Kingdom and the Soviet Union – to possess nuclear weapons, while the rest promise not to try to get them. Second, they say that if nuclear weapons are essential to security, as all three nuclear weapons states declare, why should non-weapon states be denied access to the same sort of security? Third, staying outside offers them useful political leverage. It can be used to persuade the weapons states to supply conventional weapons to non-signatories in the hope of dissuading them from following the nuclear route. This particular argument has been used effectively by both Israel and Pakistan.

While the six non-signatories remain determinedly outside the NPT, there are some inside it who pose as great a danger. Libya is one, with a record of supporting guerrilla struggles throughout the world and a desire to carry more weight than its modest size warrants. According to Israeli intelligence, Iraq is another. In 1981, unimpressed by the fact that Iraq was a signatory of the NPT, Israeli fighters destroyed the Iraqi research reactor at Tammuz, sold to them by France.

For all its faults, the NPT is a useful treaty which many believe has done something to slow the pace of nuclear proliferation. But, it has yet to be put seriously to the test, and much of its apparent success may be credited to the fact that for the past ten years few developing countries have been seriously in the market for nuclear power stations. If this were to change, and the situation eventually arose where as many as 100 states around the world possessed the reactors from which nuclear bombs might be made, then it is very doubtful the NPT could keep the floodgates closed. Some optimists argue that a world in which many countries possessed nuclear weapons would be stabler than the world we know today – but that is not a proposition most people would want to put to the test.

Assailed by this trio of problems – economic failure, environmental hazard, and nuclear weapon proliferation – nuclear power faces a crisis. Almost all the optimism of the early 1950s has evaporated. The idealists, who turned from the atom as a weapon of war and tried to satisfy their consciences by developing the peaceful atom, have been replaced by a new generation of idealists who abhor the peaceful atom almost as fervently as the military one. The Chernobyl accident – the one that 'couldn't happen' – has stripped the last pretensions from the nuclear salesman's patter. Given this gloomy outlook, is nuclear power not doomed to decline and ultimate extinction?

Analysts who study the industry are reluctant to write it off just yet. 'I don't think the nuclear industry will be knocked out everywhere,' says the energy analyst, Colin Sweet. 'It will only be affected in a country where a political decision is made to close down a programme. After all, there is a lot of money at stake. The nuclear industry is too politically and economically embedded in many countries, particularly those with nuclear arms interests.'

For many countries, the decision will obviously depend on what alternatives are available if nuclear energy is abandoned. The United States, with its huge coal, oil and gas reserves, can afford to abandon the atom without running a serious risk. But countries that lack indigenous energy sources, like France and Japan, have to make a more difficult calculation. Economic and technological growth is dependent on assured energy sources – without them our lives would ultimately be reduced to bare subsistence. And in spite of a minority who talk nostalgically about the 'return to nature', or seek to embrace low technology, most people would find this change intolerable. Faced with a choice between nuclear energy and darkness, there is little doubt which the majority would choose.

Without energy, we would have no way of running cars, trains or planes. We would have nothing to power the tractors, drills and cranes we need to make buildings. We would have no electricity for televisions, radios or telphones, for cooking or for lighting. As physicist Sir Fred Hoyle puts it: 'Energy is more important than money.'

So, in a world of declining oil resources and discredited nuclear energy, what should we do to ensure proper energy-generation on which our civilization rests so heavily? The answer, for all the bland simplifications of fervent anti-nuclear campaigners, is extremely difficult to discover.

Quite simply, every alternative energy source has its drawbacks. Solar and wind power technology are feasible but generating plants have such low output levels that a medium-sized plant would require massive tracts of land and would spoil vast areas of our already threatened environments. Wave and geothermal power (energy from hot underground rocks) are still technologically unproven, while fusion power (the controlled release of energy from the combining of hydrogen isotope atoms at extremely high temperatures) will require many decades of further research and development.

In addition, the more traditional energy sources all suffer from disadvantages. Oil and gas resources are not limitless, while coal-fired generating stations have severe environmental problems, sending clouds of sulphur and nitrogen oxides into the atmosphere. These oxides fall as acid rain and do considerable damage, destroying trees and killing fish. Fossil-fuel plants are also increasing the amounts of carbon dioxide in the atmosphere, which may one day cause climatic changes, together with flooding from melted ice-caps.

So what is the answer? Anti-nuclear campaigners make a number of claims. They point to the vast sums of money spent on nuclear research – Britain alone will have committed an astonishing £6 billion to its fast-breeder reactor project at Dounreay in the north of Scotland by the end of the century. Were such funds to be spent on alternative sources of energy – wind, solar, tidal, wave and geothermal – there is no knowing what the results might be. Equally, there is no guarantee that major breakthroughs would occur – a useless energy source will remain useless, regardless of how much is spent on it.

Other observers believe the solution lies in the improvements that could be made in traditional technologies. In America, the latest coal-fired stations have been built to new, efficient standards. At the same time there has been a drive to improve the conservation of energy by encouraging consumers to use electricity more efficiently. The process has involved a major shift away from large capital investment on power plants. Eventually, however, new generating plants will be needed to replace ageing power stations.

Future coal plants would have to be fitted with expensive filters for removing sulphur and nitrogen oxides – and these will increase power-generation costs.

One relatively new idea, developed in Britain and now being applied in Sweden, is the technology of fluidized bed combustion. Plants using this technique burn coal, but in a way that does not produce damaging oxide gases. Similarly, combined heat and power schemes, so called because they use the waste heat from power stations to heat houses and factories instead of simply venting it up stacks, are considered highly promising by some.

None of these is a soft option, nor guaranteed to fill the gap which would be left by the abandonment of nuclear power. The best immediate strategy could be summarized as 'coal plus conservation' – new, clean, coal-burning stations combined with real energy conservation measures. In the longer term some other technologies may be needed, even though coal itself is not in short supply. Fusion may eventually provide a more acceptable form of nuclear power than fission, though a working plant based on fusion is still a very long way off.

For its part, the nuclear industry has a simple answer: 'Don't panic.' Nuclear accidents are not catching and we should not allow Chernobyl to rush us into hasty judgments, they argue. But given the extent of the accident and the strong public reaction to it, there must be doubts whether the industry can manage yet another of its Houdini-like escapes from an impossible predicament.

The chances must be that in the history of nuclear power – short, chequered, but never dull – the Chernobyl disaster will be seen as the beginning of the end. Nuclear power is not yet dead, nor even necessarily dying; but the optimistic hopes that attended its birth have perished one by one. At Chernobyl the last of these – the hope that nuclear power could be safe, and clean – died along with the courageous Soviet firemen in a withering blast of radiation.

Nuclear power is simply too demanding a technology for fallible men – too demanding in care, in wisdom and in vigilance. The poisonous wastes it will leave behind have a lifetime far longer than any human culture has survived. The dangers are of a nature and a magnitude which exceed any other human activity. Faced with these daunting problems, can nuclear power justify a future as a major source of energy for mankind? On the evidence available, the answer must be no.

Major references

Brown, Lester R., Chandler, William, Flavin, Christopher, Postel, Sandra, Starke, Linda, and Wolf, Edward, *State of the World*, Norton, 1984.

Blix, Hans, Director-General's statement to the board of governors of the IAEA, 21 May 1986.

Burn, Duncan, *Nuclear Power and the Energy Crisis: Politics and the Atomic Industry*, Macmillan, 1978.

Centre for Science and Environment, *The State of India's Environment 1984–85*, New Delhi, 1985.

Council for Science and Society, *The Acceptability of Risks: The logic and social dynamics of fair decisions and effective controls*, CSS, 1977.

Curtis, Richard, and Hogan, Elizabeth, *Nuclear Lessons: An Examination of Nuclear Power's Safety, Economic and Political Record*, Turnstone Press, 1980.

Department of the Environment, *An Incident leading to Contamination of the Beaches near to the British Nuclear Fuels Ltd, Windscale and Calder Works, Sellafield, November 1983*, Department of the Environment Radiochemical Inspectorate, January 1984.

Devell, L., Tovedal, H., Berstrom, U., Applegren, A., Chyssler, J., and Andersson, L., 'Initial observations of fall-out from the reactor accident at Chernobyl', *Nature*, vol. 321, pp. 192–3.

Evans, Nigel, and Hope, Chris, *Nuclear Power: Futures, Costs and Benefits*, Cambridge University Press, 1984.

Francis, John, and Albrecht, Paul (eds), *Facing Up to Nuclear Power: A Contribution to the Debate on the Risks and Potentialities of the Large Scale Use of Nuclear Energy*, St Andrew's Press, 1976.

Gorbachev, Mikhail, television address, 14 May 1986.

Gowing, Margaret, *Independence and Deterrence*, Macmillan, 1974.

Hall, Tony, *Nuclear Politics: The History of Nuclear Power in Britain*, Penguin, 1986.

Health and Safety Executive, *The leakage of radioactive liquor into the ground, British Nuclear Fuels Ltd, Windscale, 15 March 1979*, HSE, 1980.

Health and Safety Executive, *Report on the Silo Leak at Windscale*, HSE, 1980.

Holdgate, Martin W., Kassas, Mohammed, and White, Gilbert F., *The World Environment, 1972–1982*, Tycooly International, 1982.

Hughes, J. S., and Roberts, G. C., *The Radiation Exposure of the UK Population: 1984 Review*, National Radiological Protection Board, 1984.

Lean, Geoffrey (ed.), *Radiation: Doses, Effects, Risks*, United Nations Environment Programme, 1985.

Lean, Geoffrey, *Rich World Poor World*, George Allen & Unwin, 1978.

McPhee, John, *The Curve of Binding Energy*, Farrar Strauss & Giroux, 1974.

Marshall, Sir Walter, 'Talking about Accidents', paper to the IAEA International Conference on Nuclear Power Experience, Vienna, September 1982.

Montefiore, Hugh, and Gosling, David (eds), *Nuclear Crisis*, Prism, 1977.

National Radiological Protection Board, *Living with Radiation*, NRPB, 1981.

Nero, Anthony V., *A Guidebook to Nuclear Reactors*, University of California Press, 1979.

Patterson, Walter C., *Going Critical, an Unofficial History of British Nuclear Power*, Paladin, 1985.

Patterson, Walter C., *Nuclear Power*, Penguin, 1983.

Royal Commission on Environmental Pollution, sixth

report, *Nuclear Power and the Environment*, HMSO, September 1976.

Saffer, Thomas, and Kelly, Orville, *Countdown Zero*, Putnam (New York), 1982.

Semenov, Boris, *Nuclear Power in the Soviet Union*, IAEA bulletin, vol. 25, no. 2.

Semenov, Boris, Information about the accident at Chernobyl; its consequences and measures initiated, address to Board of Governors of IAEA, May 1986.

Smith, Joan, *Clouds of Deceit: Britain's Bomb Tests*, Faber, 1985.

Stockholm International Peace Research Institute, *Nuclear Energy and Nuclear Weapon Proliferation*, Taylor & Francis, 1979.

Stockholm International Peace Research Institute, *The Nuclear Age*, MIT Press, 1974.

Tame, Adrian, and Robotham, F. P. J., *Maralinga-British A-Bomb: Australian Legacy*, Fontana (Australia), 1982.

Taylor, Peter, 'Chernobyl: the Long Term Consequences', *New Scientist*, No. 1058, 15 May 1986.

United Nations, *Report of the United Nations Scientific Committee on the Effects of Atomic Radiation, Supplement No. 45 (A/37/45)*, New York, 1982.

United Nations Scientific Committee on the Effects of Atomic Radiation, *Sources and Effects of Ionizing Radiation*, United Nations, 1977.

United Nations Scientific Committee on the Effects of Atomic Radiation, *Ionizing Radiation: Sources and Biological Effects*, United Nations, 1982.

Wilson, David, *Soviet Energy to 2000*, the Economist Intelligence Unit, 1986.

Index

238

Shultz, George, 129
Sicharenko, A., 171
Sinowatz, Dr Fred, 221
Sizewell nuclear reactor, 54, 109, 159, 160, 224
Sjostedt, Per Olof, 117
Skiyerov, Vitali, 6-7
Sloan Kettering research centre, 199
Smolensk nuclear plant, 7-8
Socialist Industry, 93.
solar power, 229
Solzhenitsyn, Alexander, 80
South Africa, 226
Soviet Academy of Sciences, 176
Soviet air force, 172, 174-6, 185
Soviet Council of Ministers, 118
Soviet Life, 5-7, 13
Soviet State Committee for Hydrometeorology and Environmental Control (USSR), 135
Sovietskaya Rossiya, 170, 178
Speakes, Larry, 120, 161
SPOT, 123-6, 128
SPOT Image Corporation, 123-6, 131
spy satellites, 118, 119-20, 121-3
Stalin, Joseph, 74, 78, 81
'Star Wars', 176
Stewart, James, 103
Strauss, Lewis, 60
strontium-89, 30
strontium-90, 24, 30, 48, 55, 86
Styrer, Kurt, 152
Sweden, 115-17, 118, 128, 148-9, 158, 159, 174, 196, 207-208, 209, 230
nuclear programme, 70, 221
Swedish Defense Research Institution, 117
Sweet, Colin, 222, 227-8
Swierk, 138
Switzerland 153-4
Système Probatoire d'Observation de la Terre, *see* SPOT

Szuroes, Matyas, 144

Tahiti, 68
Tammuz, 227
Tarapur nuclear plant, 70-71
Tass, 136, 174, 186, 197
Tatar autonomous republic, 8
Taylor, Peter, 160
Telyatnikov, Leonid, 9, 105-106
Tennessee Valley Authority, 220
Terasaki, Paul, 197
Third World nuclear programme, 70-72
Thornborough, Dick, 73, 95
Three Mile Island, 5, 8, 35, 64-6, 73, 77, 95, 97, 138, 191, 212, 222
Time, 64
Times, The, 157
Totem I, 58-9
Trino Vercellese, 152
Trud, 7
Truman, Harry, 60
Turmodin, Andrei, 170

UCLA, 197
UK Nuclear Power Co., 109
Ukraine, 1-14, 136, 142, 167-93, 195-197, 204-206, 209, 211
see Chernobyl
United Kingdom, 155-60
atom bomb programme, 50-2, 58-9
nuclear emergency plans, 158-60
United Kingdom Atomic Energy Authority, 33-4, 88
United Nations, 208
United Nations Scientific Committee on the Effects of Atomic Radiation, 210
UPI, 126, 127, 128, 162, 187
uranium, 11, 19-21, 23, 27, 29, 42, 48, 133, 216-17
uranium enrichment, 49
uranium miners, 29, 83

ABOUT THE AUTHORS

Nigel Hawkes is the *Observer*'s diplomatic correspondent and author of several books on computers, scientific instruments and nuclear energy.

Geoffrey Lean is the award-winning environment correspondent of the *Observer*. He is the author of *Rich World, Poor World* and editor of *Radiation: Doses, Effects, Risks*, an authoritative UN report.

David Leigh, the *Observer*'s chief investigative reporter, is currently Granada TV's Investigative Journalist of the Year and the UK newspaper industry's Reporter of the Year.

Robin McKie is science correspondent of the *Observer* and author of several books on nuclear energy.

Peter Pringle, an *Observer* Washington correspondent, is the author of *The Nuclear Barons* and *SIOP: An Analysis of the US War Plans*.

Andrew Wilson, the *Observer*'s associate editor and Moscow correspondent, is the author of *The Bomb and the Computer*.

DATE DUE